What It Means to Be a Teacher

The Reality and Gift of Teaching

Michael Gose

Rowman & Littlefield Education
Lanham, Maryland • Toronto • Plymouth, UK
2007

Published in the United States of America
by Rowman & Littlefield Education
A Division of Rowman & Littlefield Publishers, Inc.
A wholly owned subsidary of The Rowman & Littlefield Publishing Group,
Inc.
4501 Forbes Boulevard, Suite 200, Lanham, Maryland 20706
www.rowmaneducation.com

Estover Road
Plymouth PL6 7PY
United Kingdom

British Library Cataloguing in Publication Information Available

Library of Congress Cataloging-in-Publication Data

Gose, Michael, 1946–
    What it means to be a teacher : the reality and gift of teaching / Michael Gose.
        p. cm.
    Includes bibliographical references.
    ISBN-13: 978-1-57886-612-0 (hardcover : alk. paper)
    ISBN-13: 978-1-57886-613-7 (pbk.   )
    ISBN-10: 1-57886-612-X (hardcover : alk. paper)
    ISBN-10: 1-57886-613-8 (pbk.   )
    1. Gose, Michael, 1946– . 2. Teachers—United States—Biography.
3. Teaching—Anecdotes. I. Title.
    LA2317.G625A3 2007
    371.10092—dc22
    [B]   2007021809

Manufactured in the United States of America.

For Chris, my son-in-law, who has been such a great source of encouragement, ideas, inspiration, support, resources, help, friendship, and company.

Contents

Foreword

Don Cameron

Almost everyone believes they know how to teach school. I'm not sure if that's because on the surface teaching seems to be such an uncomplicated profession, because teachers work with children (how tough can that be?), or just because, having had the experience of attending school oneself, the average person takes on a pseudo-sense of familiarity with the education process. Whatever the reason, the country is full of non-teacher "experts" who feel free to bloviate about teaching and teachers without a scintilla of firsthand knowledge.

The truth, of course, is that teaching is an enormously difficult undertaking, one that requires the insight of a philosopher, the balance of a tightrope walker, the patience of Job, and the uncommon ability to get inside the minds young people (a daunting task for any adult). More than all of that, teaching calls for the remarkable ability to transfer knowledge from one human being to another in a setting that most often includes thirty or more other people.

Teaching is not a choice between science and art. It is both—and much more. Some teachers, particularly newer ones, bask in the intellectual command of subject matter without possessing a clue as to how to transfer that knowledge into the brains of their students. That's because effective teaching is a whole lot more than simply announcing what you know to other people. Teaching mandates getting students, by hook or by crook, to actually learn and assimilate the material being taught. In order for teachers to accomplish that job successfully they can't assume anything; they can't be boring; they can't race ahead of their students' readiness to learn; they can't be too solemn, or too corny, or too pedantic, or ignore each student's inherent ability. They can't be too strict or too lax. They can't be too rigid; nor can they simply wheel freely. They can't afford to establish a comfortable and informal camaraderie with their students while failing to get them to measure up to acceptable and appropriate standards.

In this excellent book, *What It Means to Be a Teacher*, Michael Gose uses his experiences as a teacher to educate all of us. Through the use of anecdotes and stories about things he and his students experienced during his teaching career, Gose provides insights into not only what and how his students learned, but how he personally and professionally grew from each of those experiences. He clearly and cleverly conveys to the reader what every good teacher knows: that a meaningful learning experience for the student(s) is also a meaningful learning experience for the teacher. Gose lucidly and entertainingly conveys to the reader how those experiences come in a variety of forms that are not always neatly packaged or planned. Occasionally, learning experiences induce embarrassment and self-doubt—or at least self-examination—before the lesson is learned.

Michael Gose obviously not only cares about the art and science of teaching; he cares about the people—the young minds—that come under his tutelage. In this book, he exposes a variety of individual and collective student learning experiences and is not reticent to relate how feelings of uncertainty or inadequacy can sometimes strike the teacher. If you are at all interested in the reality of teaching; if you want to learn about a teacher who is devoted to education and young people as he also copes with the education bureaucracy, this is a book for you. If you are curious about what it's really like to be responsible for educating a room full of eclectic students, this is a book for you. Within its pages, you will find the joy, frustrations, rewards, and self-analysis of what it means to be a teacher. Read, enjoy . . . and learn.

Acknowledgments

My wife, Janice, daughter, Creedance, and son-in-law, Chris, as always, deserve my greatest thanks. I am especially indebted to Tom Koerner and Paul Cacciato at Rowman and Littlefield for their encouragement, direction, and editorial help in seeing this book to completion. I was thrilled Don Cameron was willing to write the foreword for my book, and hope that readers find my book merits his fine foreword. Rabbi Zev Schostak graciously encouraged me and gave me permission to include his poem, "In the World of Tomorrow," and former students Denise Navarra and Raul Munoz allowed me to also use their poems in this book. I am also most grateful for the early readings and reviews by Lisa Kodama, Russell Lee-Sung, Charles Chang Park, Kris Janati, and Hannah Punzalan Housley.

I am deeply indebted to the countless teacher-students and student-teachers who have made my career and personal life both challenging and rewarding. Miss Hartman, Mrs. Coleman, Mr. Daly, Professor Owen, and Professor Eisner were conspicuously instrumental to my academic career. But in writing this book, I have come to a much deeper appreciation of how each and every teacher was vital to my growth as a student and as a teacher. The same must be said for each student whom I encountered. I hesitate to mention even one name here for risk of ignoring someone who has equally touched my life, and often the lives of my family members. At least for symbolic reasons, however, I want to include some names. My solution to my own dilemma is to recognize the names of the teachers and students who have also become a part of my wife's core group of friends.

Those with whom I have taught among this group include Larry Giacomino, Jill Forester, Mark Mallinger, Bob King, and Maria King. Those
among this group who were my former students include Jeannie Spitler,
Tanja Carter, Charlie Park, Chris Grimm, Paul and Brooke Begin, and our
daughter, Creedance. I am especiallly indebted to Estelle and Junius Gill
for their inspiration and wisdom. And I would be remiss not to mention
the great friendship and inspiration of Raquel Alvarez, Bill, Billy, and
Gabby Grimm, John Ellis, Tami Snow, Naomi and Taliah Snow-Ellis,
Wendy and Bill Aisley, Alaleh Azarkhish, Todd Leslie, and Zal Smith. The
names in the book have been changed mostly to protect the guilty, but
Patti Aboud, Larry Giacomino, Art Walsh, Dorothy Bettencourt, Monte
Steadman, Nick Leon, Bob Fernandez, Joe Cattarin, Chuck Short, and Joe
Randazzo are the real names of some of the heroes. While my emphasis
is on individual students, all the tenth-grade English students at the be-
ginning of my career, and the real Heidelbergers of 1985–86, demand special mention.

Along the way my teaching-assistant, Erin Shitama, provided great
help with the manuscript. Bob Escudero, Susan Cox, Genny Moore, and
Tyson Gosch were not only patient, but gracious as well, in providing assistance throughout the process of writing and publishing.

Introduction

I believe the impulse to teach is fundamentally altruistic and represents a desire to share what you value and to empower others.

—Herbert Kohl

[I doubt] the possibilit[y] of our ever arriving upon an enduring definition of what it means to teach.

—Philip Jackson

Most teachers I have known seldom wonder aloud about the true
meaning of teaching . . . [they are] too busy doing what they have to
do.

—Philip Jackson

In writing this book on what it means to be a teacher, I have sorted through
a myriad of memories, often as painful as they are joyful, of former incidents, vignettes, stories, students, and classes. Naturally my recollections
don't occur to me in any chronological order. I notice that I'm apt to remember moments of awkwardness far more often than when students and I
aced some classroom activity. I remember the sister who told her brother, on
a field trip, that she was going to sock his face in; the football player who
ran the wrong way with a fumble; the junior high student who accidentally
exposed himself to the student body in the school Christmas play; the student teacher who I finally told could change his student teaching assignment

so long as he didn't want a letter of recommendation from me; and the student I screamed at for interrupting a special performance. I remember moments more than years, individual students much more than classes, and most of my early teaching experiences better than I what I did last week.

That my memories are usually of events and encounters that stand out from the ordinary alerts me to the difficulty of my challenge: to present what I've found in my long career, what it truly means to be a teacher. The realities of teaching are most noteworthy because of their commonness, their regularity, their persistence. Looking back at the ordinariness of a life spent as a teacher, I must nevertheless conclude that it has also been a spiritual, metaphysical, and transcendent experience.

Yet having recognized my debt to students and their inspiration, which give such meaning to my teaching, I still find my mind countering this strong affirmation with the painful memories of the frustrations, trivialities, interruptions, conditions, and injustices that invariably accompany life as a teacher. I remember guest teaching at a high school, "performing" one of my rare lectures, and two custodians walking into the classroom with a ladder (twice in that one period and with no explanation) to fiddle with the clock on the classroom wall. That would seem Kafkaesque except for the fact that such interruptions are commonplace, at least in public school teaching. There are countless such difficulties: not enough textbooks for all students, materials the students can't read, shortened school days, the challenge of reaching students on Mondays after holidays, capricious administrators. A teacher's list of legitimate pet peeves could run on for pages. But this is all related to the point I want to make about specific memories being tied to context, as the context of teaching is incredibly important to what it means to be a teacher.

Thus the paradox of teaching is that, on the one hand, a teacher is invariably involved with the sublime; on the other hand, teachers are confronted daily—no, hourly—with minutiae, trivialities, interruptions, nuisances, and frustrations. The teacher must simultaneously perform a sacrosanct and priestly role and also work like a laborer, performing minimum-wage tasks. After spending nearly all of my entire adult life as a teacher, I've found, upon great reflection, that I've come to some accommodation and perhaps even wisdom about what it means to be a teacher. Teaching is indeed a gift. One is a gifted teacher, not because of an inherent skill set, but because of what one receives or is gifted with as a teacher.

My sure conviction is that there is an intimate relationship between the particular experiences of teachers and the significance of teaching. St. Thomas Aquinas (1948, p. 137) says, "For this reason truth is defined by the conformity of intellect and thing. For to know a thing in general, and not in particular is to have an imperfect knowledge of it." The reality of what it means to be a teacher is about both the particular and the general. The bulk of this book addresses the particulars of teaching. But I also believe in and feel that I have experienced the general and transcendent essential, even spiritual dimensions of teaching, the dimension that recognizes the sanctity of the teacher-student relationship, a divine connectedness. Though this book starts with the particulars of teaching, it ends with a much shorter reflection about the general, *essential* qualities of what it means to be a teacher. Certainly I have wanted to emphasize both the realities and the ideals in all of my deliberations about teaching because they are intimately related, not separate.

ORGANIZATION OF THE BOOK

The much larger first part of this book emphasizes existential realities and the second, brief part is concerned with the fundamental essence of what it means to be a teacher. The difference in quantity of text does not reflect my true emphasis. The second and final part is based on the existential realities of the first part. In the first twelve chapters in the first part of this book I attempt to capture the experience of teaching and thus what it means to be a teacher. These twelve chapters reflect the realities of teaching that I think all teachers face. These twelve chapters are independent and can certainly be read out of order. The order in which I do present them, however, represents the following flow of ideas:

Every teacher has a *first year* with its special stories that come with being a novice (chapter 1). It is not coincidental that most popular books on teaching are about teachers' first years. It's the year with the momentous clash of ambition versus reality and the year when a teacher makes her or his most memorable mistakes. Further, all teachers face certain *job conditions* that are inevitable and that shape what it means to be a teacher (chapter 2). Teachers also inevitably face a great deal of *failure* and have to make decisions often without key information about students (chapter

3). On the other hand, while never being able to be too proud, teachers do have clear-cut *successes* (chapter 4). Despite the inherent limitations to the role of a teacher, *"But I am a teacher"* is the theme of chapter 5. Much of what it means to be a teacher gets worked out in the teaching of *the curriculum* (chapter 6). However, it is generally the *special people* one meets that enrich life as a teacher (chapter 7). It's a good thing there are the special people because some *administrators* and their abuse of authority can often frustrate and try teachers' souls, and challenge teacher morale (chapter 8). The conundrums, the *dilemmas*, the perceived problems that have no obvious solutions, have special influence on defining, individually, what it means to be a teacher (chapter 9). What it feels like to be a teacher is highly circumscribed by the ambivalence that comes with being so frequently *honored and betrayed*, often on the same day (chapter 10). Apropos of chapter 11, I've read that in the United States most policemen, by far, never fire their guns in the course of their careers. Well, most teachers are never assaulted, but like policemen, there's always a concern about potential danger that leaves every teacher with an underlying sense of being *vulnerable* (chapter 11). Finally, in terms of what it means, existentially, to be a teacher, the unexpected *joys* along the way are some of the truest rewards for being a teacher (chapter 12). These twelve chapters lead to the inescapable conclusion that experiencing life as a teacher is likely to lead to growth as a human being.

The stories that I present in the first part of the book describe the kind of experiences a teacher has; the stories emphasize "the existence" a teacher experiences. While I think I still have the heart of a tenth-grade English teacher, I deliberately include my full range of "teaching-learning experiences" from preschool to graduate school, teaching, "social work," and administration. The second part of the book (chapter 13) tries to distill those chapters into the *essence* of what it means to be a teacher. While liberal use is made of both exposition and storytelling, I attempt to use words to paint, in pronounced strokes, an overall impression of what it means to be a teacher.

In fact, the reader might do just as well to skip the introduction and go straight to the stories in each chapter, to return later to the rationale contained in this introduction on why I had the audacity to write such a book and how I've organized my thoughts on what it means to be a teacher.

When you have finished this book, I have a special request: My ardent desire is that thousands of teachers will become co-authors with me, that they will add their stories to the blank pages in this book and give this book to others, whether to family, or to the school or public library. Please consider adding your stories.

Writing Prompts for Teachers to Add Their Own Stories to This Book

Chapter 1: A story from my first year of teaching

Chapter 2: A nightmare story about the conditions of teaching

Chapter 3: A classic story about a time I clearly failed, my fault or not

Chapter 4: I have to admit—this was a huge success on my part

Chapter 5: This is a story where I probably succeeded as a human being

Chapter 6: One was one of the best classes I ever taught, where all systems were go, full steam ahead

Chapter 7: In my Hall of Fame of former students, I especially remember this student

Chapter 8: Let me list just some of the ways administrators drove me to distraction

Chapter 9: In retrospect, I was actually quite proud about how I resolved this teaching dilemma

Chapter 10: This is something a student wrote me that I treasure

Chapter 11: This was a time I was most anxious, even a bit afraid as a teacher

Chapter 12: One of my favorite stories that suggests the joys of teaching

Chapter 13: In essence, this is what I feel it means to be a teacher .

ARGUING MY CREDIBILITY

I think the credibility I might bring to writing this book is that I'm like most every teacher in that I:

- collect, even hoard things
- am a bit absentminded
- am a bit vain, but not about looks or possessions

- have outside interests
- love teaching, yet love the breaks
- prefer being relatively "time rich and money poor"
- like to read
- am a bit impatient (despite the superior value patience is presumed to have to a teacher)
- feel a bit underappreciated and underpaid
- have nightmares, especially near the opening of a new school year, that I am in a classroom and have lost complete control of what is going on
- am always on the lookout for stuff I could teach, and collect thirty to thiry-five copies of anything that I might eventually use with a class
- distrust administrators, commissions, mandates, test results, experts
- insulate myself from most educational fads
- am a little younger in attitude than I might otherwise be, primarily because of the influence of students
- am a bit odd, but then a teacher needs to cultivate a personality that holds students' interests
- never get used to the amount of failure I experience as a teacher
- am, despite discipline problems that might be an influence toward conservatism, relatively more flexible, liberal, open-minded than I would otherwise be
- complain too much, but that complaining is also a sign that I care, that I'm committed to my place and my profession
- probably learn more from my mistakes than my successes
- enjoy teaching more when I center my attention on my students not just the subject matter (which doesn't mean I don't regard my subject matter)
- am more of a nerd than I'd ordinarily like to admit
- take myself a little too seriously but exceed the six laughs a day that are supposedly the average number of laughs an adult should have in a day

Why am I qualified to write this book? It's too audacious a claim to think I'm truly qualified to write a book on such a grandiose topic as what it means to be a teacher. But it's my sensibilities rather than my many official credentials that lead me to try. When my friend and fellow teacher, Larry Giacomino, won the school's teacher of the year award, I asked him how he felt about the recognition. He answered that he thought he should have won the award every year. I feel that way, too, and hope most other teachers feel that way as well. I treasure a line I heard from my favorite author, James Herndon. He was teaching with other renowned teachers in a summer program for teachers when he overheard a "regular" teacher remark, "Hell, I can teach that well." I like that. As Norvel Young, former president of Pepperdine University, often remarked, "There's no competition among lighthouses."

A BOOK WRITTEN ON BEHALF OF TEACHERS

Why hasn't there ever been a book truly written for teachers? There are books ad nauseam about all the problems, yet somehow two and a half million of us or more do continue to go to work until we retire from the job. There are a few wonderful books about charismatic teachers, most of whom felt driven out of the profession. Did all the good ones leave? The good and more resilient are still there, doing well, thank you. And most of the rest of the books on education are niche books about specific issues that do not pertain to most teachers and their lives in classrooms.

This is meant to be by example a book about the countless regular teachers, good teachers, a book that collects enough images, stories, anecdotes, laughs, and comments to give an overall impression of what it actually means to be a teacher in America. Although they are inevitably my stories, I emphasize that it's because these stories are like the stories that all teachers have that this book is important, not because of me.

I want to have written and compiled a blessed book about teaching. I want the book to present the most and best representations of what it truly means to be a teacher. I do not want it to be about the exceptions, which tend too often to be negative, or when positive, unrealistic. I want the book to be about good teachers and good teaching, which is much more general than commonly realized.

In order to be successful, the book needs a timeless point of view about teaching. I intend for the book to capture the positive, the humorous, the good. In it, I will emphasize the most commonly shared positive images of teachers, with a gentle commentary on the extent to which those images are real. The book will be 100 percent about the 95 percent of teaching that is positive. Commissions, titles, presidents, tragedies, and headline news stories are not the substance of daily life behind the closed doors of the classroom; they are not a big part of the daily life of teachers and their students. Even the most obvious social developments—including mainstreaming and immigration, the rising number of single-parent families, increased drug use and poverty—are only of limited significance. For every year teachers concern themselves with twenty-five to thirty-five individuals who are each different in a class that has its own unique personality. This book is looking for the timeless qualities of what it means to be a teacher.

This book has the modest goal of being the primary representation of teaching in modern America. While commission reports, educational fads, news reports, and professional jargon have been pervasive in the public discussion of education, they are not representative of 99 percent of the reality of teaching. Even the very real problems of teaching are misleading in that most of what goes on in classrooms involves teachers and students performing in a give-and-take manner that is fairly typical of how all people live out their days. The exceptions become newsworthy, but are not very typical. Day by day, decade by decade, increasingly competent teachers reasonably handle increasingly complicated expectations with significant educational results for less than the reasonable cost for mere day care.

The following compendium—call it an album, scrapbook, chronicle, or collection—contains a record of what it means to have been an American teacher. Like life, it is full of laughs and tears, successes and failures, heroes and occasional villains, insight and mystery. I have written this book to capture what it means to have been a teacher in America. As the Reverend Jesse Jackson has said, "A text without a context is a pretext." I think that my wife, Janice, has a sure and true understanding and perspective on schools. Four points that she regularly makes are most instructive, and help us establish a context for this text:

1. Teachers are the people we have entrusted with our children. If we say our children are so important, how is it that we allow teachers to accept this charge with such inadequate support and such modest pay? (One of our own answers, by the way, has been how lucky it must be for the teachers who has a student like our child.)

2. Schools are one of the last (safety) nets to catch everything from physical and medical problems to behavioral and emotional problems—all for about the cost of day care, with an education thrown in as well.
3. Schools are a microcosm of the macrocosm. Schools will have all the same kinds of problems the society has, whether it is smoking and drugs or insecurity and aggression.
4. Institutions are no better than the individuals that comprise them. Much can be forgiven if and when the teachers and school have your child's best interests at heart.

INNER CALL

I never heard any inner call to be a teacher, although I had heard that teachers are supposed to hear such a call for that to be their true vocation. In retrospect, after several decades of teaching, I can see more clearly that (1) growing up I was rather dense about prospective careers and the future in general; and (2) the insistence of my roommate (Marty Ernster) that I should be a teacher was in fact something of an inner call. Apparently he saw with clarity what I could not see for myself. But having started teaching, I did want to become as good at it as possible. I think it was Philip Jackson who said, and I'm sure with some truth, that most teachers are too busy teaching to worry about what it means to be a teacher, I have spent my whole career thinking about what it means because I was so eager to truly become one.

I want to say again that in trying to write the telling and representative stories about teaching, it's not me that's in any way important. I'd focus on my exceptional (as opposed to rather ordinary) stories, if that were the case. My point in this book is to try to find what's general about teaching among my own experiences; I am seeking those stories that I think are most representative of what other teachers experience.

St. Thomas Aquinas says that you cannot know the general except in relationship to the particular. That's what I want to capture here: the general essence of teaching through a discussion of the particular experiences. I want my account about what it means to be a teacher to be an enjoyable and affirming read for teachers, and for it to communicate this reality as well to concerned non-teachers, whether they be students, parents, or community members. And I am very hopeful that thousands of teachers will sufficiently identify with my stories that they will write their own stories in the blank pages provided in this book. If they then donate these particularized books to their school or community libraries, together we will create a library legacy all over the country that celebrates what it means to be a teacher.

TWO GENERATIONS IN SCHOOL

In first grade I was confronted with a flash card that read either "grandmother" or "grandfather." If I had had more time I probably could have sounded it out. But with flashcards there is an expectation of immediate recognition. I guessed. I guessed correctly. I was elevated by Miss Moss to the highest reading group.

In second grade a bunch of us were out of our seats. Mrs. Dagwood (yes, that really was her name) was not pleased. I dropped to the floor and scooted back to my desk on my hands and knees. Everyone else got in trouble. Was it possible she hadn't seen me?

In third grade Mrs. Rawlings told me she would go ahead and recommend me for the fourth grade even though I was still iffy on the multiplication tables. In fourth grade Miss Heath wrote on my report card, "Mike continues to talk too much." I also sat next to a bookcase and secretly purloined *The Song of Roland*. I read it while carefully hiding it in my lap.

In fifth grade Mrs. Hartford was my truly favorite teacher. I suspect it was because she, of all my elementary school teachers, seemed to like me the most. In sixth grade I didn't get along with Mrs. Goss, but she would recite *The Highwayman* to us by heart. And I could go on, listing the ups and downs that defined individual years in my life as an individual student.

As to my daughter's school experiences, in first grade the teacher wrote on her report card that she had trouble with paragraph development. In second grade, she went to school in Heidelberg, Germany. In third grade she read more books of anyone in her class. And she adored her teacher.

In fourth grade my daughter quit doing her math homework. It was a decision not unrelated to her relationship with her teacher. Fifth grade was unmemorable. Sixth grade was at a middle school. One of her teachers had been my student. Again, I could go on listing those features that stand out as highlights in my daughter's school years.

The major similarity between my experience and my daughter's—and I contend the major similarity of all classroom experiences from 1950 to 2007—is that a teacher and about thirty students did academic work in a self-contained classroom, and much of the success was related to the relationship of the teacher and the particular student. Between 1950 and 2007, of course, the resources available to teachers became far richer, and students now have a lot more influence in the teacher-student relationship.

Near the end of his book *Notes from a School Teacher*, a book that I treasure, Jim Herndon (1985, p. 156) says, "But I go down to my classroom. Room 33. Inside it, I close the door, and all of the above, most every concern brought up in this book, falls away."

While all the supposed changes in education are certainly worthy of a different book, I believe, and I contend here, that what it means to be a teacher is primarily dependent upon what goes on behind those closed doors. While the external factors are so often alienating, the teaching in relationship with students is fraught with meaning. That relationship is what is most essential to what it means to be a teacher.

Part 1

EXISTENCE

Existence, n. 1. Reality as opposed to appearance. 2. Reality as presented in experience. 3. Being with respect to a limiting condition or under a particular aspect. 4. In existentialism: the condition of a person aware of his radically contingent yet free and responsible nature. (*Webster's New Collegiate Dictionary*)

1

First-Year Teaching

And gladly wolde he lerne, and gladly teche.

—Chaucer

EVERY TEACHER HAS A FIRST YEAR

Yes, every teacher must have a first year. That first year is often fraught with rude awakenings and silly mistakes that are both memorable and (with time and recovery from the anguish and pain) humorous. For those teachers who enter the profession immediately after their undergraduate years, the first year is particularly difficult because it's also the time of transition into full adulthood. Further, it's incredibly difficult because most of us who have spent so many years as students think that because we recognize good teaching we'll automatically be good teachers. But it's not that easy.

I remember my first year well, even though it was over thirty years ago. I was starting my teaching career at Fields High School, a comprehensive, "multicultural" high school in East San Juan, California.

ORIENTATION

Certainly the beginning of the school-year orientation that was offered my first year of teaching didn't do much to prepare me. I had two days of orientation before my first classes began. The first day was for new teachers only. We were a small group. Each of the onsite administrators lectured us in turn about our areas of responsibility—fulfilling our supervision assignments, recording student absences, turning in student grades, checking out textbooks, calling for a substitute, understanding insurance coverage, making sure payroll information was complete, and so on.

Of the administrators, the principal made the best impression. It was his first year as a principal, he told us. He'd finally made it up through the ranks. He had been a math teacher, football and baseball coach, and vice principal. He told us he was particularly proud of his coaching record. He told us, "We won the district's first county championship in football. I used to put in long, long hours. Finally my wife told me it was her or football. I couldn't have both. [He paused.] I thought about it a long time and decided to keep her." He received an appreciative laugh, so he decided to repeat the now-rehearsed story in the orientation for all teachers the next day. In fact, we heard a carbon copy of the entire speech the next day—a day that was otherwise forgettable.

As to my part in the preparation for the new school year, I remember I had grandiose plans for the year. These, in fact, were not any more helpful than the principal's orientation had been. I might as well have made no preliminary plans at all.

FALSE START

The first day of classes fell in the middle of the week. This was a real break for me, since by Friday I knew I had to scrap all the plans I had made all summer. At the beginning of each class period I introduced myself by announcing my name and writing it on the board. "My name is Mr. Gose," I announced. I had been well warned that I should expect students to call me "Mr." Students expect teachers to perform a formal role in the traditional high school. Young teachers who invite students to use their first names give students wrong cues—regardless of the other merits of students calling teachers by their first names.

I continued: "My name sounds like, 'ghost,' with no *t*, but is spelled like goose with one *o*." I said this as if I were reading from an encyclopedia. I didn't mind students chuckling at my reference to "ghost" and "goose." I knew from my own seventeen years in school that students would butcher my name. I didn't want my students to derive too much satisfaction from "accidentally" mangling my name as they "discovered" funny ways it could be pronounced; I didn't want them testing me this way to see how sensitive I might be. When I was in high school we loved to get teachers' goats, especially teachers who had trouble with students, by saying their names in some indirect and clever manner to see them get mad. (For example, we loved to call out the first name of our humorless wrestling coach, "Elmer," when we knew we couldn't get in trouble for it.) I apparently achieved the desired effect with my students, because I never had a problem with the use of my name.

The first day I lectured and asked a few questions, which for the most part were not answered. I also tried to memorize the name of every student the first day. I didn't succeed, but I did know all the names by Friday. I had been told correctly by several experienced teachers that the best way to insure good discipline and a good start was to know and be able to call students by their first names as soon as possible. There is a profound difference between calling a student's name and saying, in effect, "hey, you," when asking him or her to behave.

At the beginning of my presentation to my first class I told the students about myself, that by the time I had graduated from high school I had attended thirteen different schools. A few students admitted they had been to as many as seventeen schools even though they were still only in the tenth grade. I think my transience was something most of my students identified with. I also told them about my academic background at Occidental College and Stanford University. A few students "oohed" in approval of Stanford. I proceeded to outline the course for the students in some detail; I covered the entire green blackboard with notes. I explained to them what I thought at the time was a major innovation. Instead of studying literature chronologically or page by page through the text, we were going to study themes, like "Man (sic) and His Environment," "Man (sic) in Conflict," and so on. I then had to repeat a similar lecture four more times to my other classes. The lecture did not improve through repetition. Fortunately no one paid much attention, and the following week — when I realized that most of my students could not read at grade level and I would have to change all my plans — no one seemed to notice that I was not sticking to my original plans. If they did notice, at least they didn't complain,

In truth it was not only the official curriculum that was to be tested.

STUDENT-ADMINISTERED TEACHER TESTS

Students do not waste any time testing a new teacher, and they often find ways not covered in a teacher preparation program. The following examples offered by Bert, Melinda, and Olivia were typical of what students did to find out what they wanted to know about their teacher.

Bert

Did you ever see the robot Hymie on the old television show *Get Smart*? Hymie always did exactly, that is literally, what he was told to do. If they told Hymie, "Knock it off," Hymie would knock it—anything—off of something. If they told Hymie to "shake a leg," Hymie would shake his leg. I asked Bert Carnes to turn around. Since he was sitting sideways, he naturally turned to the other side. I asked him to turn all the way around; Bert turned all the way around and ended up facing exactly the same direction he had been facing originally. I asked him to make the front edge of his desk parallel with the line created by the desks in front of his; he turned his desk exactly backward, which meant the edge *was* parallel to the line. Wisely, I think, I laughed and let him sit that way. He hadn't been insubordinate, he had been funny. But it had also been a test, and as far as my class was concerned, I had passed.

Melinda

The facts that I was twenty-one and that I dressed reasonably well (for a teacher) meant I did not have to be handsome to be popular among many of the female students. At first, it was flattering, and I admit that I kind of liked it for a while. Later I realized it was a burden. During my honeymoon stage as a new teacher, Melinda Grey made me the "best" offer:

"Mr. Gose, are you married?"

"No."

"Who does your cooking?"

"I do."

"Are you a good cook?"

"No, I'm terrible."

"Would you like me to cook for you?"

Food is always presumed to be the way to a man's heart, isn't it?

Olivia

Olivia was a very comely lass with large breasts who knew how to embarrass me, although I doubt that was all she had in mind. When Olivia needed help, she would come to my desk and show me the writing she was doing. As I looked at her paper, she would gradually start leaning against me. She was subtle enough so I could not exactly ask her to quit because she could have feigned shock that I would have thought such a thing. My first response was to slide away from her on my seat. Once she finally went too far and I literally slipped off my chair as I moved away from her. I reprimanded her with a sharp, "Olivia!" To my surprise and relief that finally ended the problem.

THE PECULIAR PROBLEM OF
THE YOUNG, BEGINNING TEACHER

The beginning teacher who starts right out of college has some special crosses to bear. He or she is often asked what he or she is doing in the faculty restroom. As a beginning high school teacher I had difficulty being admitted to even the junior class social in the gym or to the school football games. Being called Mr., Ms., Miss, or Mrs. for the first time, we novices are often briefly confused when our name is called. We momentarily wonder, has our parent suddenly dropped into our school? Mr., Ms., or Mrs., used with our last names, are what our parents are called, not us.

ROOKIE EXCESSES

Even a lot of ideas for the classroom that seemed good at the time, and even "worked" to some degree, seem at best naïve in retrospect. One assignment I gave my students stemmed from my Boy Scout background. I asked them to go home and do a good deed, without mentioning that they were doing it as a school assignment. The oral reports the next day were exciting, descriptive, varied, and funny. Two kids had done the good deed (like washing dishes without being asked) and had had their allowances raised. Quite a few more students were asked to do more chores around the house after their good deed, as their good-deed recipients were so grateful. Almost every good deed was met with some reaction of amazement or bewilderment.

The students' oral reports were good. My department chair, a traditionalist in a humorless kind of way, was not as impressed as I was with the results. For the time being I didn't worry about that criticism. After all, my students were suddenly more active, more involved. I felt great. Many of my students were reading and writing effectively, many for the first time. I doubted there had ever been such a good first-year teacher. I had even greater ideas for the next couple of units.

In retrospect, I wonder, how could I have been so foolish and naïve? My success here led me on a string of rookie excesses. I can hardly justify what I "inflicted" on favorite students like Steven, Olma, Reed, and Ty. Mistakes are made, but beginning teachers tend to make up in enthusiasm what we lack in experience.

Steven and Olma

One of the clearest indices of a school's official concerns is their range of printed forms. Unless you consider report cards a reward, none of the forms (and there are usually dozens) are favorable to or supportive of students. Tardy slips, truancy forms, referrals, failure notices, absence slips, warnings of various types—these all sanction, control, and intimidate students. There were absolutely no forms for students' files to commend them for excellence in any field. Starting to feel rambunctious and to test my limits after some early success with my classes, I decided to revolutionize the system by giving *positive* referrals to Steven and Olma, simply because their work in my class was so good. How nice, I thought, for Steven and Olma and their counselors to experience a referral for outstanding work and behavior. I did not get the effect I sought. So it gose.

"Steven, I have a referral for you," I announced. I made sure I said it pleasantly, but Steven just froze, terrified. There was a buzz in the room.

What had he done? *What'd he done?* Obviously, nothing that was not excellent. Steven's face turned red and I was suddenly a little embarrassed. Since the referral was a form that would go into a student's permanent file, I had written a commendation under the referral category of "other." I thought his counselor might be happy to have a student come to his office who was not in trouble.

I did the same thing with Olma and got the same reaction. But then, I shouldn't have been surprised by their reactions. Even as a teacher, if I got a note to see the principal I assumed I had done something wrong, even though I would have no idea what it might have been. Those of us on the treadmill of success have internalized what Jules Henry has called "the essential cultural nightmare": the "fear of failure" as well as the "envy of success." Thus Steven and Olma immediately ended my "practice" of sending students to the office for good behavior.

Reed

Some work that I assigned students was amusing, and also got some of my students into a bit of trouble. I think particularly of Reed Alvarado, who always had bad things happening to him. In a creative writing unit I recommended that my students go home and do something they usually do, only this time do it blindfolded. Reed went home and washed the dishes. Without the use of sight he broke a dish. His mother was not pleased.

This was not the only time Reed was in trouble with his mother. Trying to teach some skills in memorization in case the student ever had anything he wanted to memorize, I asked them to memorize Langston Hughes' "Motto": "I play it cool/and dig all jive." Reed's mother thought he had joined a secret gang, and called the principal. More trouble for the rookie teacher.

Ty

I was guest teaching a unit on drama for Montgomery Stedfast, also of the English Department. One of the students, Ty Addler, played third base on my frosh-soph baseball team. Ty was one of the really humorous characters in the school and he could really dish it out. Upon completion of the drama unit I announced a "final" exam. I introduced it soberly that Friday, but in the end I subverted it.

I walked into the class sternly, frown on face, briefcase in hand. I set the tenor for the class by saying harshly there would be no talking. When someone raised a hand, I repeated, "No talking." The mood was set in the way teachers—intentionally or not—generally set the mood: by the way I started my class.

I passed out the test, gave the necessary instructions, and sat down deliberately at my desk. I was coming on like a Gestapo officer after having run a fairly relaxed class, and the class deferred to me. Everyone was absolutely quiet and busy at the test.

Now I should also mention that at the time I was learning this trick on how to seem ubiquitous, as in omniscient and omnipresent. I had discovered the limitations to one typical approach to student misbehavior and was exploring another approach. When, as a teacher, you notice a student misbehaving, you can look at the student, get his or her attention, and then suggest the student engage in a more positive behavior. However, with this technique, you catch only what you see. What I was learning is that if you can catch something out of the corner of your eye, and look down, around, or away, and *then* ask the student to behave, it makes it seem like you have eyes in the back of your head. Or even better, that you are ubiquitous. It's a great skill for good classroom discipline.

So about five minutes into the test, knowing full well that Ty had not moved his eyes from his paper and without looking at him, I said evenly, "Ty, just look at your own paper."

Ty immediately tried to defend himself. I looked up at him, raised my hand to say "enough," and went back to the papers on my desk. A little later I again spoke up.

"Ty, I'm not going to tell you again, just do your own work." I said it a bit more angrily this time.

"But Mr. Gose . . ."

"I don't want to hear it, Ty."

"Grumble, grumble, grumble," Ty said. He had his nose almost touching the test he was so anxious not to be accused of cheating. But seconds later I stood abruptly.

Loudly I screamed, "Ty, I said that was enough!" I pulled a pistol, actually the starter gun from the track program, from my briefcase and fired twice. God, it was funny. And only God knows what a terrible thing that was to do to someone. Ty fell back in his chair as if he had been shot.

There was absolute horror on his face, and it was the only time I have ever seen eyes like saucers.

Well, the lesson was sort of related to drama. I was making a reputation as a precocious young teacher and valuable member of the English Department, but I can't really justify what I did to Ty. And yet, it probably wasn't my worst mistake as a rookie.

MOST EMBARRASSING

By far my most embarrassing moment, one that can still cause me to sweat just remembering it, occurred somewhere around my second month of teaching. I was twenty-one teaching high school students, many or most of whom were probably more worldly than I was. I was having a lot of early classroom success and my particular lesson was going extremely well. I got caught up in it, and went beyond my preparation.

I had been teaching the elements of fiction: plot, character, setting, point of view, and theme. This particular lesson was on character. I had decided to read aloud some Mother Goose nursery stories and after each short piece ask the students about the characters in each story.

For whatever reason, these urban teenagers were paying rapt attention to my reading of these tales. They kept asking me to read more, and I believed by the looks on their faces and their poses—they were sitting forward in their desks—that they really did want to hear more stories. Some of my most reserved students were asking me to keep reading. I believed they really wanted to hear more, not just get out of whatever work might come next.

It is hard to find better examples to introduce the topic of character and characterization than the examples from nursery rhymes. Think of Peter, Peter, the pumpkin eater; Little Bo Peep, who has lost her sheep; Simple Simon; Little Miss Muffet; Jack and Jill; Little Jack Horner; Jack Sprat; Little Boy Blue; and even Humpty Dumpty. The start and middle of the lesson went so well. As I said, for whatever reason the students were enjoying themselves.

Like Icarus I was soaring—until I crashed and burned. I had caught the crest of the wave—until I wiped out. And like Superman, I was saving the world. Until I stumbled upon the kryptonite.

I turned one more page, one page beyond what I had prepared. I had gotten too taken away with myself. I otherwise would have known better.

What is it within human nature that now tempts me to relive my humiliation by baring it to you, the reader? It is not to confess that my story is politically incorrect, although you will need to recognize some tawdry slang to appreciate my folly. But I have committed to sharing my stories, even the embarrassing ones, with the goal of conveying the typical teacher's experience. Within a heartbeat of starting to read that next nursery rhyme I knew that I had erred. I turned one more page and was in no man's land. If you, dear reader, do not know why I was immediately in trouble with a classroom of precocious teenagers, I will reassure you that I once read in Ann Landers that it is good to be innocent, but not naïve.

I turned the page and started reading "The Owl and the Pussy Cat." Looking back, I felt then as I once felt when I locked my keys in my car in an unfamiliar city. In the brief moment before I actually heard the clank that my car door makes when it locks, I knew I had left my keys in the ignition. If only I could turn the clock back a split second. But I was already reading the poem.

By the first line the snickering had started and I was probably turning beet red. Yet my only thought was that if I stopped, I would acknowledge that I knew why they were snickering, an acknowledgment that I, as a beginning teacher, was not prepared to make. Disastrously, the poem began:

> The Owl and the Pussy-cat went to sea
> In a beautiful pea-green boat.

Immediately I knew I should be more than a little bit worried about the pussy cat. But bravely—no, stupidly—I read on.

By the fifth line I knew the cat was in serious trouble. The owl looked up to the stars above and sang to a small guitar. What did the owl sing?

> O lovely Pussy, O Pussy, my love,
> What a beautiful Pussy you are,
> You are,
> You are!
> What a beautiful Pussy you are!

The house came down around me. The teenage boys, I noticed, were almost falling out of their chairs as they tried, with little success, to forestall outrageous laughter. And all I could do to protect any shred of dignity was to continue reading as if I had absolutely no idea why there was such a sudden and continuing uproar of laughter.

Regardless of whatever successes I had my first year of teaching, that class was the defining moment. It was my true induction into teaching and my pursuit of the question of what it means to be a teacher. It's minimal consolation knowing that every teacher must have a first year.

2

Job Conditions

Recent research . . . do[es] show certain kinds of improvement in the occupation of teaching. In the past half century in particular, the academic attainment, age, length of teaching experience, pay, and collective influence of teachers have risen substantially. Tenure and less restrictive community expectations have given them much more economic security and private autonomy than they once enjoyed.

—David Tyack

If a doctor, lawyer or dentist had 30 people in his office at one time, all of whom had different needs, and some of whom didn't want to be there and were causing trouble, and the doctor, lawyer or dentist, without assistance, had to treat them all with professional excellence for nine months, then he might have some conception of the classroom teacher's job.

—Donald D. Quinn

OVERVIEW

A teacher's identity is especially influenced by common job conditions. Certainly any career has its set of circumstances and work conditions, but those of teaching are particularly unusual and influential. Where else does an adult work intently, day after day, with thirty other persons of a completely different age group in approximately twelve hundred square feet of space? This chapter will explore some of the ways these unique job conditions shape the lives of teachers.

THE INFLUENCE OF JOB CONDITIONS

I once wrote an article describing a teacher's "job conditions" for the California *Journal of Teacher Education* (Gose, 1996). These conditions certainly have a shaping influence on what it means to be a teacher.

Under "job conditions" I cited the research by Jackson (1969, p. 11) about how many judgments a teacher must make each day. I cited the pressure of thirty to forty people working in such a small amount of space. I also noted the isolation from other adults and the particular influence of the rhythms, the peaks and valleys, of the school year.

I noted the dramatic changes in society that have had such an influence over the nature of teaching. Since I was in college, there are now more jobs in the public than private sector, and more jobs in service occupations than in production. Since I started teaching the demographics have changed from nearly half of America's families having school-aged children to only about a quarter. There are more single-parent families than two-parent families and less supervision at home. The mandates on what to include in the curriculum have grown without anything being designated for removal. We have more diversity, more competition for students' interest, shorter attention spans, a wider variety of ability levels in the same classes, and no appreciation that the fourth-grade reading level is *not* the level all fourth-graders should be reading at—it's only the average.

No one seems to know that teachers, as a group, graduate in the top half of their college classes. The negative statistics about teachers' college rankings usually cited in the newspapers are about high school students who said they were going into teaching, not those who actually became teachers.

Such considerations are not "what it means to be a teacher," but they are conditions that help shape the identity of teachers. They are like the lathe of heaven. Such conditions as these tend to sharpen particular characteristics that we probably all have in common, to some degree, as human beings.

The amount of stimulation in a teaching job tends to bring out an ability to make quick decisions. It also, perhaps, makes us less willing to talk and interact once we get home. We are tired of communicating. Our "vacation" schedule, which is so envied by others, tends to be a necessary respite from the great activity of the teaching days. It tends to take us a long time to wind down.

Teachers tend to be ambivalent about "patience": on the one hand we are very patient with students, but on the other hand, we're impatient with bureaucracy. We irritate and annoy our families by bringing classroom issues home with us (not to mention papers to grade). We almost always have become more "liberal" than we might even want to be as we learn to accept as many of our students and as much of their behavior as we can. On the whole we become very responsible. No matter how we dress, or what kind of car we drive or music we listen to, students keep us more apprised of what's happening in popular culture than we might otherwise want to be. There's a special burden on teachers in the primary grades who, unless they're careful, start talking only in simple sentences. Almost all teachers are able to initiate conversations with a wide range of people. We adopt coping skills that allow us to withstand the constant failure we experience in the classroom, the student problems we can't resolve, the mindless decisions by administrators, and fads and mandates from sources that know little about real students.

In this chapter on the influence of job conditions, I'm going to argue for the need to include teachers in any decision-making process. Then I'm going to relate two specific characteristics that most all teachers are forced to develop: frugality and physical stamina.

THE NEED TO BE PARTNERS IN CHANGE

I love innovation. I love new ideas, being creative, finding and trying new ways of teaching. Yet one of my pet peeves is the constant mandate to change schools in any number of ways, and the *tone* of the professional conferences and in-service training sessions designed to bring about such change. Certainly I'm not for stopping that kind of energy when it has the potential to be positive. My point is rather that most teachers sitting through (often suffering through) these conferences and training sessions, which barrage us with presumed solutions to chronic problems, already know more than we can act on. What we need most is more time and more energy rather than mandates made by groups that do not have input from teachers. Be assured, there is no such thing as a teacher-proof curriculum. When we close our classroom doors, it's still pretty much up to us. We have to live daily with the results. So we'd like to be at least partners in implementing constructive changes in teaching and the curriculum.

NECESSARY FRUGALITY

Because of our modest incomes, teachers live lives that are almost invariably shaped by frugality. Perhaps God wanted to explore the idea of "frugal" when he or she created teachers. Compared to the people of the world—and for that matter all the people of history—teachers lead comfortable lives. Most all teachers have medical benefits, a retirement program, and enough money for basic expenses. But we do not have much disposable income. One of the biggest "problems" with our one great job condition—180 days of work a year, 185 days theoretically off—is not that we aren't making money the 185 days we have off, but that we have all of those days to spend the modest income we make in the 180.

Our limited incomes tend to make us more money conscious than we would prefer to be. We tend to know where every dollar, if not every penny, goes. I remember, and it is a troubling memory, one particular time that my wife came to school to pick up my paycheck. Before the day was over, she had deposited the check, bought groceries, and allocated the remaining cash. When she split the cash I knew instantly we were short twenty dollars. And we were. And I knew that my wife had not miscalculated at the grocery store. It had to have been a bank teller error. Sure enough, the bank teller had twenty dollars too much in her drawer at the end of that day, and we received back the twenty dollars due to us. Yet I would much prefer to think I wouldn't have noticed the twenty. By necessity teachers are careful with their money.

Despite this, teachers are very generous with their students. The researcher in me has always wanted to calculate the amount of money teachers, especially elementary school teachers, contribute out of their own pockets to school programs. I would not be surprised if it is over one billion dollars a year. In addition to classroom expenses, teachers are the first line of adults students approach for candy sales, magazine drives, car washes, and walk-a-thons.

Having taught high school, when I began teaching elementary school I confess that I had some resentment of elementary school teachers for their conspicuous generosity with their students. Being on a fixed budget, I was not prepared for the students' expectations—fueled by their previous school experiences—that there would be periodic prizes, treats, and even parties throughout the school year.

Yet I learned through the example of countless other teachers that you may calculate the cost, but you do what is required regardless. A teacher must disregard the costs of cleaning bills that come with messy art projects and messy students. The pastel chalks and sticky watercolors, the playground of clay and mud, and the sticky fingers come with the territory. (The IRS should consider the cleaning bills a professional expense or a charitable contribution.)

There's one particular twenty-dollar expense that stands out in my mind more than any other. (In my defense, I'll point out that early in my career twenty dollars put a lot of groceries on the table, especially fruits and vegetables from the farmer's market, which we drove to to make our money go as far as possible.) As an elementary school teacher, one of my favorite field trips was to the local public library. At the library, the students would have the opportunity to obtain library cards. Then they could check out a specific number of books. If the library was close enough, we'd go back two weeks later to return the books.

When we made this one trip that I'm thinking of, long-playing albums were still in use. Record albums were, of course, very fragile. (As I write this, one of my college students, who is very into music, tells me albums are still produced in small quantities for aficionados like himself because of their superior sound quality. Whatever happened to 8 tracks?)

On this one day, I got all the necessary permission slips from my students and we headed out on our walking field trip to the library. I led the group and my wife, Janice, shepherded the group from behind. It wasn't a hot day, nor a cold day. The students were entirely cooperative along the way. No dogs approached to distract or bite us. No homeless persons accosted us. No lawn sprinklers wet us. The librarians were nice. It might have been a perfect day. But Carolyn wanted to check out a jazz album along with her books. Children were not allowed to check out records. She asked me to check it out for her.

"But please, Mr. Gose!" she said.

"Carolyn, you know that we are only here to check out books," I replied.

"But please, Mr. Gose. My dad would love to hear this album. It's his favorite singer," she pleaded.

And what went through my mind as a teacher? Well, as a teacher, I wanted to take every opportunity to encourage positive children-parent relationships. And I suspect this was particularly important for Carolyn. She was absolutely not an abused child in any way, but she showed signs of slight neglect around the edges. She showed signs of some attention, but not enough, for example, she was clothed adequately but with no accessories. She was a very nice child, a likeable student, special.

And I somehow knew beyond the shadow of any doubt that she'd drop and break the record before we even got back to school.

"Carolyn, if you lose or break the record, they fine you $20.00." I told her.

"Mr. Gose, don't you trust me?" she responded.

Undoubtedly I paused, hesitated, probably swallowed hard.

"Mr. Gose, if I lose it, or break it, my dad will pay for it."

You do what you have to do.

"Okay, Carolyn. If it's that important to you, I'll check it out for you." Which I did, on my own library card.

An unwritten law of teaching is that you trust students until you have reason not to trust them. An unwritten law of life is that the adult who makes the decision is responsible, not the nine-year-old.

As Carolyn stepped off the first curb in leaving the library, the slight jolt propelled the record out of its sleeve and into the crosswalk. The album shattered into small pieces.

What do you say to your student?

"Carolyn," I said, "you know the line about 'don't cry over spilt milk'? Well, don't cry over a spilt record album." So she didn't. She did insist on taking the album cover home to her father to prove the goodness of her heart.

It was a good thing the bank had admitted that error previously and given me the twenty dollars they had owed me, so I could honor my own error and pay the library such an amount. For I certainly never thought I would receive the twenty dollars from Carolyn's father that Carolyn was so insistent he was good for—and I never did. I had known that the results were inevitable, and yet as a teacher, knowing all that I knew, it was an investment I had to make that day for Carolyn.

As teachers we invest our time, our emotions, and our money, and none of this threesome should be undervalued or unappreciated.

PHYSICAL STAMINA

What I have wanted to suggest in describing some of the mundane conditions that shape the lives of teachers are the elements against which a teacher must strive in being a coward or hero. This is my quintessential story about striving against the conditions of teaching. Is it a story of a heroic failure or of cowardly luck?

Having taught both elementary and high school, I can say without chance of contradiction that high school teachers have no true appreciation for the physical stamina being an elementary school teacher requires. Whereas I am otherwise writing about what it means to be a teacher at any grade level, this story is a special tribute to the millions of elementary school teachers who have held their posts. Joseph Conrad's Lord Jim was both a coward and a hero, but in that order. I fought and won many a valiant battle against my human frailty, and then on one otherwise unnoteworthy day, I left my post. It was not without travail.

I was a fourth-grade teacher with a cast of usual suspects. In this class I had Harold, who knew all there was to know about the Civil War—even why it's not referred to as the War between the States—but who generally refused to do his math. I had Theresa and Delman, who were siblings. It was one of two times that I had siblings in the same class who were not twins; they were born virtually nine months apart. Theresa was older and more mature, except perhaps when it came to her interaction with her younger brother. Theresa once took exception with Delman on a field trip to the General Motors auto plant, and pronounced to him that she would, and I quote, "sock your face in."

The class also had two all-school athletes, one male, one female, as well as a classic nerd who couldn't play softball, basketball, or baseball. He was generally despised among his male peers because of his apparent lack of athletic prowess and his shockingly high math scores (until the fateful day when I took the class bowling—more on this story in chapter 4). And there were the couple of dozen other students who had the advantage or disadvantage, according to your point of view, of passing through school without being noted as such memorable characters.

With this group, I wouldn't have been so concerned or worried if I had had to slip out of class for a few moments for whatever reason, even though slipping out of class for *any* reason is strictly and entirely against the law. Every student must be specifically, not generally, supervised by a credentialed teacher, who got credentialed by going to school for years and years and by passing an FBI fingerprint test. And undoubtedly, unless you, the reader, are or have been an elementary school teacher, you can scarcely imagine any circumstance that would cause a teacher to abandon his or her class.

This one year, however, my worries about meeting that circumstance when I may need to abandon my class—leaving myself open to losing my job, losing my teaching credentials, and leaving my school and district vulnerable to an expensive lawsuit—were compounded by the fact that Parker was in this class. Parker was the scariest kid I have ever seen. Parker was scarier even than Stinky, who used to threaten to beat me up every day when we were in eighth grade (until he found out I could play second base).

Like most teachers who stay in the profession, I have a great, if naïve, belief in our ability as human beings to overcome the worst of circumstances, including learning disabilities, being physically challenged, and desperate home conditions. But I was dismayed for Parker. An otherwise healthy-looking child, he was born with two shades of coloring on his face. The result was that he looked like he was wearing a mask, which evoked the image of a villain wearing a ski mask to conduct heinous crimes. When anyone saw Parker for the first time, he or she almost always shuddered. Parker, naturally enough, noticed this reaction, and while it may not have been healthy for him, it did give him a sense of power over others from a very early age. No teacher could command the immediate attention and "respect" that Parker could.

While working to bring out the good side of Parker, the prudent teacher kept one eye on the class and one eye on Parker. Parker was not to be trifled with, or left entirely to his own resources. Yet, as is becoming increasingly apparent to you the reader, I was going to leave him unsupervised with my class of thirty otherwise unsuspecting nine-year-olds. I was going to leave the class. I was going to abandon them.

Junior high and high school teachers cannot truly appreciate the predicament in this story because they teach in forty-five to fifty-five minute blocks. They get five minutes between each class, a nutrition break, a lunch break, and a prep period. An elementary teacher gets no breaks between classes, and if she or he has playground supervision that particular day, she or he may go as long as four hours without a break. Teachers' unions periodically try to improve these job conditions, but do not underestimate the pressure on teachers, especially elementary teachers, to persevere over extended periods of time.

And we have yet to include another fact of life teachers face: children carry, seemingly on a daily basis, every communicable disease known to man, and probably a few not yet known. While spending most of their youth building up their own immune systems, these children share the colds, viruses, flu, pink eye, and worse with their teachers. Teachers, meanwhile, generally believing in the perfectibility of man, manage to overlook the great potential physical harm these students are generously sharing with the one adult in their custody.

All of this is, of course, a very long buildup to my actually very short story about abandoning my class to the fates. It is a story that all but the elementary school teacher will tend to deprecate. But it is told with the greatest sincerity. And for me, the moment I will describe is frozen in time.

The best clue that trouble was coming was that I was quickly emptying the tissue box that sat on my substantial wooden desk in the front corner of my classroom. No, I hadn't been crying. It was just the stuffiness of another head cold, which breeds bacteria I suppose. And this eventually affected my stomach. Which, on this rare occasion, gave me the opportunity to practice my will power, my stoicism, my mental toughness, and ultimately my bowel control.

This was one of those rare occasions in a lifetime, when one's tummy, one's belly—one's very guts—calls out to its owner in the startling voice of the exorcist that immediate attention is demanded. Emergency! Emergency! Clang! Clang! Clang! I know you have been there at least once, just probably not in front of a fourth-grade class twenty minutes until a recess that it's your week to supervise anyway. I was twenty steps away from total disaster. Mayday! Mayday! Craft going down! My eyes and teeth were aching, there was perspiration on my brow. I had queasiness, heart palpitations, knotted guts, weak knees, stark fear. There was danger ahead.

It was not a matter of my life passing before my eyes in seconds, but it was related. Life's great questions centered on: Where's the key for the faculty bathroom? Is the student restroom closer? But what if a student sees me in there? All the students should be in class, I thought. But what if the principal comes in while I'm not here? It's my first year here; I'll lose my job. How else will I take care of my family? What if Parker kills one of the other nine-year-old students while I'm gone? Can I live with the guilt? And then, the final question: What choice do I have?

There's no time to get a credentialed supervisor for my class.

Realize, reader, that all of these questions occurred to me in micro-seconds, because if I had considered them for even long seconds, the opportunity for action would have passed, so to speak.

Parker's attention was elsewhere. I moved behind the students and slipped as noiselessly as possible out the back door. How long until they noticed I was missing? I fled to the nearest facility, the boy's restroom. The quick and agile mind of my youth realized that since there was only one stall in the faculty restroom, I could not risk its being already in use.

And I made it, just in time. As I squatted on the undersized stool I experienced pure ambivalence: the relief of being where I was coupled with the dread that my career as a teacher would be flushed down the toilet as well. Probably at that very second Mr. Cockerell, the principal, had decided to pay his first visit to my classroom. Or, worst-case scenario, Parker was inflicting some merciless punishment on one of my fear-stricken nine-year-olds. My sense of time was suspended. It was like slow motion in the movies, with each click of the clock beating, beating. Thank God there was toilet paper (this was before huge cutbacks in custodial staffing). I was experiencing time without end.

Then I was back. I eased the door open. There was no sign of any other adult in the classroom, no sign of Mr. Cockerell. Not only was Parker not on top of some other student pummeling him mercilessly, but he was still at his desk. No one had even missed me. My willpower had failed me, but the fates had been kind. It was a miracle. I had abandoned my post, but I had not been caught and there were no dire consequences. No one need know. I could return to the façade that I was a teacher in control of my class. It was a comforting illusion that we rarely try to perpetuate. Plop, plop, fizz, fizz, oh, what a relief it was.

Job conditions such as this shape us as heroes and cowards, and eventually shape what it means to be a teacher.

A FAIRER ASSESSMENT OF TEACHERS

If we are going to assess teachers, and what it means to be a good teacher—or the learning experience in schools in general—we can ask certain questions.

1. True or true: No one has (or had) as good a teacher as they deserve or need (or deserved or needed) each year. Okay, the answer is true. Now, having accepted that, what about a more realistic set of questions?
2. Were almost all of your teachers in class almost all of the time when class started? How many other professions are likely to have a better record in that regard?
3. Other than relatives, how many adults did more for you from kindergarten to twelfth grade than teachers?
4. How would you like to work in a 900-square-foot office with at least thirty other people?
5. Do you know any other job that typically requires one to make twelve hundred decisions a day?
6. Would you want to go to school that long to work for that pay?
7. Would you rather have to spend as much time (as a student does with a teacher) with a teacher, minister, doctor, or lawyer?
8. Can you personally name four people who were actually harmed by a teacher?
9. Do you realize that students who were not like you may have related to the teacher with whom you did not relate or who you did not like?
10. If you had more than one teacher, you probably had a favorite and a least favorite. What percent of your teachers were basically okay? (Factor out the fact that most kids complain about anything they have to do.)

11. Percentage wise, did you complain more about your parents/ guardians or your teachers? Any employer or your teacher?
12. Was your teacher's grammar at least as good as what you hear on TV?
13. Did the teachers, as a whole, dress better than the kids at your school? Better than your grandparents?
14. Did most of your teachers know your name?
15. Did the amount of drill and rote learning you had to do compare at all to that reported in Asian schools?
16. Did you get to talk to more people your age than at any other time or place in your life?
17. Did you laugh at least six times a day at school (a healthy national average for a full day)?
18. How often did you have your own desk to sit in?
19. Were most of your teachers there almost all of the time?
20. Are you smarter than you would be if you had dropped out?

3

Failure

The vanity of teaching often tempteth a man to forget he is a block-head.

—George Saville, Marquis of Halifax

INTRODUCTION

My student teacher, Trudy Crown, captured well one vital component of teaching: "you are never prepared for the amount of failure you experience as a teacher." Research has shown that it is not unusual for a teacher to have to make twelve hundred judgments in a classroom day. One does not need to make but a very small number of mistakes in those twelve hundred decisions to have a very bad day. Some of the failures are strictly personal, with no one to blame but oneself, one's own limitations, shortcomings, or faults. Other failures are failures nonetheless, but they are due to what is unknown and probably could not be known, that is, a teacher is inevitably handling situations with students without having access to all the vital pieces of the puzzle.

In this chapter, I will present, first, some brief stories about the kind of personal failures a teacher is likely to experience as I experienced them in failed lesson plans; the failed handling of a discipline problem; and a story of failed patience. Then we'll take a look at some of the situations a teacher may face where he or she is missing some critical information.

PERSONAL FAILURES

Dope

My first two bombs in teaching were rather hard for me to cope with. The first utter failure was with the play *Dope*, from the still-popular *Scope* magazine from Scholastic. It was a dated play from an old issue, but there was a lot of action and my second-period class had a great time translating the dated slang into their own slang. With my second-period class, it was a great lesson on idioms and how times change, and we enjoyed some discussion on drugs and such, as well. After running such an excellent class second period, I was really excited about how well it would go with my fifth-period class. After all, I had a proven product. Was I surprised!

"I don't want to do this," one student said.

"Do we have to do this, Mr. Gose?" whined another.

"This is a lot of crap," said a third.

"Why don't we ever do anything good in here? This is boring," they continued.

Totally unprepared for the onslaught of criticism, I complained, "What's the matter with you guys?" and I said it rather angrily.

"It's boring," they said.

"It can't be boring. I know it's good stuff. Second period loved it."

"We ain't second period, Mr. Gose."

That stung. It was of course true, but I did not accept it right away. Down deep inside I knew it was true, but for a while, I tried to tell myself that the problem was boring students—the material had proven itself. In the end, however, that fifth-period class was a failure. Second period and fifth period are never the same.

A Unit on Rhetoric

The second disaster I took even more personally. Seven years before, I had been—like my current students—in tenth grade (though I doubt my students would have ever thought of a teacher as having once been in tenth grade). We had had a unit on semantics that had really interested me. We talked about stuff like, "No cat has five tails; a cat has one more tail than no cat; therefore a cat has six tails." Well, it was interesting to me at the time and I had kept my syllabus from my tenth-grade class. I had remembered all the activities and readings and everything and I assumed it would be a real treat for my students. I waited to use it as a trump. I planned out a three-week unit and knew I could spend even longer on the topic.

Three days later, though, I yielded in the face of my class's negative reaction and scrapped the whole thing. Just because you liked something as a kid doesn't mean today's kids or these kids will like the same thing. After all, your second- and fifth-period classes might not even agree. My past was not to be a standard of measurement. I learned difficult but critical lessons from this failure.

"The Tell-Tale Heart"

Another lesson I had to learn was about trying never to be wrong. I often read Poe's "Tell-Tale Heart" at Halloween. I'd really juice it up. I would turn out all the lights and really get dramatically involved in the story. I'd read with an eerie voice, use a metronome at different speeds for the heartbeat in the story, and have a large blue eye that glows in the dark for the story's "hideous eye." My reading ruins my voice for a couple of days, but it's really fun.

I had read aloud once already that Halloween and promised to do a repeat performance. I asked everyone who was interested to come to my classroom no later than fifteen minutes after school was out. About thirty-five students came in and, after due preparations, I locked the door as I had said I would so there would be no intruders. I started the story. About two minutes into the story, someone started knocking at the door. Since there was a "do not disturb" sign on the door, I thought the person would surely go away. The person kept pounding, louder and louder. I kept reading louder and louder. And he kept pounding on the door, louder and louder and yelling, too.

It was Del Rhames and I was sure he had better sense. I yelled for him to quit. He did not. I finished the story and ran out of the classroom. I have no idea what I actually said when I confronted him. I am confident if we had both been students it would have been one hell of a fight. I exploded, shocking myself at my own volatility. The other students just eased on home. Del followed them. The two of us were still furious. I was sure I was right, Del should not have done what he did. I could await his apology, if he ever came back to class.

But if Del had been wrong, I was wrong in how I had handled the situation. When he came in the next morning (and I was grateful he came to class the next day), I asked to talk to him outside. I apologized for the way I had acted, right out front, with no further accusation on what he had done. He apologized, too, although I didn't expect it.

I think we both got a lot out of that encounter, even though I still wish it had never occurred. Teachers should not always have to feel they are right. That is how I had always found my teachers and sure enough that was how I had acted. There were plenty of times I needed forgiveness for mistakes and it was helpful that I recognized my mistake here so I could build a bridge back instead of being self-righteous.

A Three-Letter Word

My hassle with Del Rhames was ironed out, but I was feeling more and more hassled in general. Any teacher who has ever ordered audiovisual (AV) equipment knows that the equipment never works when you most depend on it. Have you *ever* been to a meeting anywhere a temporary microphone worked right off? The microphone always squeals and groans. Then, after someone finally gets that to stop, you can barely hear the speaker.

The same holds true for tape recorders, record players, film projectors, and anything else that has mechanical parts and uses electricity in a high school AV department. This same year, my fifth-period class broke into groups and wrote a play. All week we had tried to turn it into a radio show. We tried to read the lines dramatically, added sound effects and a music background, and put it onto tape. I had brought in a tape of an old Lone Ranger radio program as an example. The first day the tape recorder didn't work. The second day the AV department forgot to deliver the tape recorder; when I finally did track it down, there was no microphone. The third day, the record player did not work. The fourth day, which was Friday, we had to finish the play. I was just too frustrated trying to patch classes together when my lesson plans didn't work out because of the equipment failures.

The students had done a *Mod Squad* play (groan, another rookie excess) and we were very slow getting it on tape because Ike Kerner kept blowing his cues. This made him more nervous and led him to blow more cues, which frustrated both me and the class to no end. But somehow my patience had seemed to hold out and with fifteen seconds remaining before the bell, the final music was playing to an end. Ike (who had been hoping someone else would make a mistake so he was not the only one) yelled out, "You blew it, you blew it!" I had not blown it, but this did ruin the last scene, and then I really did blow it.

The words just came rolling out of my mouth, so easily and quietly. It was far too late to stop them when I realized they had been said aloud. "You ass," I said. Ike turned bright red, the bell rang, the class ran out laughing. I envisioned losing my job for what I had said in class, besides what I had probably done to Ike.

Fortunately no one told on me and Ike forgave me. These kids were the ones who collected the most food on the food drives because they knew what it was like to be hungry. They understood teacher frustration undoubtedly because of their own frustrations. I idealized them too much, but most were good kids. I liked them. They accepted me despite my failures.

WHAT YOU DON'T KNOW . . .

The nice thing about the kinds of failures we've been discussing is that you can respond by teaching better lessons, handling discipline problems more effectively, and being more patient. The more perplexing problems are those where a teacher is never likely to know all he or she needs to know to resolve an issue.

Here's a series of vignettes where, some time later I just happened to find the missing pieces to a puzzle. In the situations presented here, I couldn't possibly have anticipated what I didn't know I didn't know. What you don't know won't necessarily kill you, but it is a major, if hidden, factor in what it means to be a teacher.

Mike

Let me tell you a bit about Mike. Mike was such a congenial, cooperative student, I assumed in the first few weeks of teaching that he was one of those "model" students teachers depend upon. One day, trying to make a point in class, I said, "Suppose Mike robbed a store? What would happen?" I did not consider it an even remote possibility that there could be any reality behind that statement; I did not even faintly think about that possibility. After class, Mike asked me how I knew. It had been before he had moved to this area. He hoped it wasn't in his school file. Uh oh.

So Mike had surprised me, but I still found him to be a personable student. All that kind of trouble must be behind him. He was, after all, my student now, so *shouldn't* those kinds of problems be behind him? But later, Mike came to me for help. He had a drug problem. It was clear to me that doing something immediately for Mike should be my highest priority, should be the school's highest priority. But I had to ask Mike to sit through a whole period of my class while I sent messages around to my fellow teachers—who certainly did not want to teach an extra period that day—to find a replacement so that I could deal with Mike. (Possibly I should use another word than "deal" here.) And if you wonder why I didn't send him to a counselor, you don't yet realize counselors schedule students and keep track of their class credits—they do not have time to counsel.

I made good use of the time waiting for a "substitute" teacher by pulling out the file I had assembled on drugs. I had kept every school bulletin on the drug problem and had taken a one-unit class at San Jose State, so I went to my file confidently expecting information that would help me cope with the responsibility of helping Mike. What I had were three hundred pages that described every drug, what it did to a person, and why it was dangerous. There wasn't one useful bit of information on what I should do right then, not even a good referral.

Fortunately, one of my teacher peers was very experienced in the field and gave me a phone number. Ms. Abdul took my sixth-period class (bless Hattie), and Mike and I went down to a free clinic and made the initial commitment to get him into a program and out of his particular drug problems.

How could such a nice kid develop a drug problem? Only losers have drug problems, I thought. Didn't he know it would not solve any of his problems? Mike's story was that his father had left home many years earlier. His mother had worked until failing health required her hospitalization. Mike started working full-time to help out (while still going to school), and then welfare cut some of his mother's welfare check because of the family's additional income. So Mike started pulling some overtime, too. Someone had told him one of the hallucinogens might give more insight as to what to do. Mike did not find any answers in the drugs, but he did welcome the escape.

Melinda

Rob Grey was a really personable student who was also a little rowdy. Everyone figured Rob would really do something with his life, if he survived adolescence. I have no idea how I knew Rob, other than the fact I had had his sister in my first-semester English class. I don't know that I ever taught Rob anything academically, but I did intervene in his life as an educator. Rob's sister, Melinda, had been hassling and hassled by her family ever since her father had left them. Finally, in a heated moment with her mother, Melinda left home. She bummed around for a while and then got a live-in babysitting job with an eighteen-year-old mother.

Terribly unhappy, Melinda started missing school often and dressing shabbily. She looked pale and weak. During her initial absence period, I asked Rob what had happened. He angrily told me about the fight, defending his mother. Melinda had apparently been rude, but then she was only fifteen. I assumed it would work out, but the more school Melinda missed, the more I was concerned. Melinda was incredibly stubborn, as was Rob; I guessed the mother was as well. I approached Rob near the end of a lunch period.

"What's happening?" I asked.

"What it is," he replied.

"What did you hear from Melinda?"

"Nothing. And that's okay with me."

"I'm worried about her," I continued.

"Yeah, I guess I am too. But she had it coming. She's so stubborn. She really hurt Mom."

"How do you think she feels about it?"

"I don't know—hadn't thought about it."

"Do you think you could do anything about it to get her back home?"

"That's her problem."

"I know Melinda respects you; she's told me. Sounds like your mother does too. Sure wish you'd try. Do you mind that I asked?"

"Nah, that's cool."

"Later."

"Later."

Despite my good intentions and possible good influence on Rob and his family, I was still only scratching the surface in terms of what was going on with them. I saw the conflict between Rob and Melinda and tried to do something. I hadn't pretended to know the causes. But I was, nonetheless, shocked when I found out several years later that the live-in situation was an affair between the adult mother and a minor, Melinda. It was this that was causing the intensity of the family conflict.

POTENTIAL HASSLES LURK EVERYWHERE

Tim

Vandalism is a problem not just in schools, but in airports and stores, at McDonalds, and in your neighborhood, no matter where you live. In schools, of course, it's a special problem, not only because of the immaturity of adolescents, but because of the concentration of people. As an administrator I tried never to take vandalism personally — it was bad enough to have to deal with the problem anyway. But petty vandalism was sometimes enough of an irritant to exasperate me personally. I was already exasperated one day when I found two kids I knew well, Tim D. and Vance J., kicking in a locker that I knew was already damaged, having been kicked in before. I came up from behind them. In retrospect I should have figured they didn't think they were doing anything wrong, because they were scarcely concerned by my approach. That lack of concern on their part in and of itself probably set me off.

"What in the world do you think you're doing?" I asked angrily.

"Kicking off the door." Tim kept kicking. I was incensed.

"Stop it!" I felt like grabbing him, but of course I didn't. I'll rarely touch a kid, only to break up a fight in progress. Tim quit for the moment.

"What's the problem?" he asked belligerently. "It was already broken."

"Go to my office, both of you," I demanded.

"Why should I? I'm not doing anything wrong." Tim responded. Vance was quiet throughout the incident.

"We go to my office so we don't embarrass each other in front of anyone," I insisted.

Reluctantly Tim and hence Vance agreed to go. We walked across the quad and into the back door of my office. I broke one of my cardinal rules. I didn't split them up. I knew them both well. Tim had excelled in the reading lab I had personally instituted and even helped teach during the first weeks of its inception. Vance lived in the house behind me where I lived in Fontara. I gave him rides to school some days. This seemed an easy problem to handle in the confines of my office, so I didn't separate the two. I kept them together. Further, I was in a hurry, and the problem wasn't that big of a deal. I knew both kids. I wanted to scold them; have them take it; and dispense with the situation. I knew the locker had already been broken. I let them both sit next to each other across the table from me. It was a grievous mistake.

"So what did you think you were doing?" I asked—another poor question that invited one of *Mad* magazine's Snappy Answers.

"Kicking in the locker door," Tim answered petulantly.

"Doesn't it seem to you something is wrong with that?" I queried.

"No, it was already broken," he responded.

"Isn't it possible you were doing further damage?"

"Nope. It was already broken."

I can't recall the exact dialogue thereafter because I broke my second cardinal rule and got mad. We both got mad, and Tim stormed out of the office. I admit I was angry and might have missed some cues as to Tim's behavior, but I was not prepared for how quickly volatile he had become, and how irrational. I was mad too, but not nearly to the same extent.

"Vance, what happened?" I asked, puzzled.

"I don't know Mr. Gose. Sometimes Tim's like that," Vance answered.

I've had enough experience with conflict to know this was something unusual, something special, and I was a bit worried. I hadn't pressed Tim that hard. I hadn't insulted him. He had been out of line kicking the locker and his deed required administrative follow-up. But it wasn't a big deal. His behavior worried me. I couldn't imagine what he might do next, and I didn't want it to simmer with him. I called his home and his mother answered. I briefly described what had happened and decided to go talk with her in person. I also knew Tim's older sister, a senior, who was in my work experience program and a "model" student. I drove to their upper-middle-class, split-level home. I wondered vaguely if Tim might not now vandalize my home. Mrs. D. greeted me cordially.

"Mrs. D., I was really surprised by Tim's behavior. It wasn't my intention to incite him. I really don't think I did anything to cause such a strong reaction."

"I'll have to hear Tim's side of the story, but I don't doubt your story. Did you know he had a lot of problems with the assistant principal down at the junior high?"

"No, I didn't," I replied. "I only known Tim because of the great job he did in the reading lab."

"Well, I'm surprised Luna [the junior high school] didn't tell you. He and Mr. Crumb didn't get along at all. They even wanted Tim to see a psychiatrist about his attitude toward authority."

"I'm really surprised by that," I said.

"It was an ongoing problem—three years. I really don't think it was all Tim's fault either, but I know he does have something he hasn't worked out."

From my point of view, Mrs. D. was being extremely fair. She would not pass judgment on Tim until she heard his side of the story, nor would she hold him blameless as other parents have at other times. About that time Tim walked in, paused, and went into the kitchen.

I ran the risk of my home visit blowing the incident out of proportion (home visits being as rare as a house call by a doctor these days), when in fact my goal was to keep a lid on whatever had happened.

"Mrs. D., you are welcome to talk to Vance, too, if you think it would be helpful. I'd trust him to give you a fair story."

"No, I'll just talk to Tim, but I imagine he thought because you are a vice principal, you must be like Mr. Crumb, so he acted like he did with Mr. Crumb," she said.

"I certainly can't speak to that, but I want Tim to be responsible in some way for the door he kicked in, even if it was already broken. I think he might fix it as a suitable consequence. But I also don't want to make this a bigger issue than it already is. Tim's done well at the high school; I want him to come back tomorrow. If you or he would like to talk more, I'd be glad to meet with you."

"Thank you, Mr. Gose."

Tim came back. We put the issue in the past. We were more wary of each other thereafter. And I know that if his friend Vance hadn't been there at our confrontation, if Tim hadn't had to posture toughness in front of a peer (even though we all knew each other already), this incident would never have occurred. I've never kept students "in trouble" in the same room together since. The social dynamics are quite different when peers are together.

In this case, much more was going on with Tim than met the eye. When a student puts him- or herself in a position to get caught, there's often more going on than meets the eye. Revelations of past problems should be private, and I should have had him by himself in my office.

Football

I probably haven't yet told you what a great athlete I am. I haven't told you because, regrettably, it's not true. Imagine then my trepidation when members of the high school football team, which had been ranked third in Northern California, asked me to play tackle football with them after school. Harry Boyd, who became a front-page star at San Dimas State, and Whitford Ronson, who was even better but who had problems getting to school, invited me to the afternoon game. The only other teacher asked was Steven Hendrickson. I knew I was crazy, but it was such an honor to be asked (I'm serious), I played anyway.

There were about nine players on each team and they lined me up as a defensive rusher following the opening kickoff. I had played flag football in college intramural leagues, but tackle? Without equipment? I decided they would have to respect me for giving what I had, and I was seriously willing to give it. God only knows why. It was a crazy idea.

My first play from scrimmage was something less than glorious. Because there were only nine men on each team, their defensive line was not close together. At the snap of the ball, I put a good move on their tackle and stepped quickly between him and their guard. For a moment I felt cool. But their blocking halfback, Mick, introduced me to the "forearm rip." I had heard the term before, but this was the first time I had ever had the opportunity to experience it firsthand, so to speak. Mick laid me flat out on my back. He was a little embarrassed for having destroyed me so easily and helped me up.

Whitford Ronson was the captain of our team. He thought it was awfully funny, but nonetheless, dedicated to winning, he moved me to a linebacker position, where maybe I could at least stop a pass. The next few plays were run away from me and then I helped out on a gang tackle. I did my best to make it look like I was giving it my all, while at the same time doing everything possible to avoid getting hurt. While I was standing around thinking about it, I decided what I needed to do was pull off one great play and then play half-assed for the remainder of the game. Next play I got my chance. I was playing right linebacker and noticed our defensive right end was split too far out from our line. I somehow instinctively realized Harry Boyd was going to get the ball and cut through the hole between our rushing guard and end. Sure enough—their first halfback out of the backfield took our corner-back deep; their left end took our safety deep and Harry, on a delay, ran right through that hole. And there I was. It was my chance for greatness. And I knew all I had to do was hit this superstar low to bring him down. Glory awaited me.

There is one particular difficulty in a 160-pound novice trying to hit a younger man, who can use his hands and who can bench-press 400 pounds, low to bring him down. Harry stuck a straight arm into my head; my arms flailed and my neck sank into my shoulders. I missed the tackle. Harry romped the last forty yards easily for their first score. Glory had passed me by, at least for the time being.

Neither of the quarterbacks from the varsity team had showed, so our team was without a quarterback. I surely was not going to volunteer to play quarterback, even though I did give a lot of thought to George Plimpton, the writer and nonathlete of some fame who tries pro sports and writes about them. After we had tried to move the ball unsuccessfully several times, Whitford suggested I try the quarterback slot. I did used to win a lot of sand-lot games throwing to receivers who were good enough to catch about anything thrown in their general direction. Down 7-0, I brought the team back with a 76-yard touchdown throw. Sound impressive?

On my first play from scrimmage, they blitzed. Every member of their team ran at me, screaming. (Thanks guys!) I was playing quarterback from the shotgun formation, back away from the center, and about as soon as I got the ball, the first three guys hit me. But I didn't panic—I simply didn't have time. I ducked under them just like I had seen Roman Gabriel of the Los Angeles Rams do in the Coliseum and somehow I came out of the stack standing up. The only teammate near me was Whitford, who was about two feet away. I dropped the ball, as much as passed the ball, to him and Whitford ran 76 yards for our first touchdown. Not exactly a 76-yard bomb from a strong right arm, but as the sportscasters say, you can't tell the difference in the box score. I'll take it.

With the little added confidence I'd gained, I threw for a couple more touchdowns. I was really feeling great about being out there. It was almost like I knew what I was doing. Then, I decided to fake a pass and run around right end. It worked beautifully at first, and as I got around right end I had our all league end, Tim Priest, to block for me and only a small safety to beat for a long touchdown run. I just assumed Tim would block for me so I concentrated on running as fast as I could. Tim, however, apparently figured I would cut behind him. The safety hit me head on and my head hit sharply against the ground. Fortunately he knocked me all the way out of bounds because I certainly fumbled the ball. But it had been a nice gain and the guys in the huddle gave Tim a bad time about his blocking, so I was still feeling cool even if I did ache. Near the end of the game, I was reminded again not to take my success too seriously. Whitford called the play with a pitch (lateral) to me. Whitford took the hike and pitched to me. I tried to sprint left and did so only to notice all the other guys on my team were going right. Wham. I was blasted. It was the last play of the game. They carried me to the locker room.

Thinking about the incident years later, I am still not sure why Hendrickson and I played. Latent machismo, I suppose. Even later, actually ten years later, one of the student football players put the game in its proper perspective. At his ten-year reunion, Tim Priest, who had not made a block for me, explained why we played even without pads: "When you've got that much energy, you've got to do something." He also told me what I had been too naïve to realize before: "I can tell you now, 90 percent of the students were loaded. How else would they be crazy enough to play tackle without pads?" I suspected I finally knew why Tim Priest missed his block on what should have been my touchdown run. I had been in the dumb class and there had been so much about school life I was slow to pick up. I think I deserved an A for effort, but probably an F in figuring out what was really going on.

You can believe me, I was not trying to be one of the gang by playing football. I have never been accused of that particular shortcoming in my life. But I do think, despite my naiveté, that both the students and I gained greater respect for one another because of that game, even if they had been loaded. In the classroom, the teacher is in full control: he or she sets the norms, gives the directions, evaluates the student performance. On the football field, Harry and Whitford set the norms, gave the directions, and evaluated the performance. In a way, they did a far better job than I often did in the classroom. There was no harsh criticism when I, or any of the other players, failed at a task, only encouragement and perhaps a quick point of instruction. They gave the directions, but were open to suggestions and adapted their strategies accordingly. The individuals knew how well they had performed and there was no need for formal evaluation, but I am confident that if I, or another player, had needed feedback regarding performance, Harry and Whitford would have given it accurately. The key was that we had a common task to work toward, unlike in school where everyone does only his or her own work.

I argue that teachers learn the most from their failures. My original title for this book was "F." As I mentioned in the beginning of this chapter, Trudy Crown observed that teachers are never prepared for the amount of failure they experience on a day-to-day basis. As suggested by several of the stories in this chapter, teachers make moment-to-moment decisions and rarely have all the information they might need to make the most prudent decision. However, somehow teachers survive their failures and learn from them. Learning from failure is becoming one of the most defining characteristics of our job.

4

Success

What we do know about the retention of what is learned in school is, alas, not very encouraging. Research tells us that the bulk of it disappears from memory almost before the ink on the pupil's report card is dry. Yet some of it obviously endures. And even the portion that is forgotten leaves a residue of some sort that has a way of changing the person in whose mind it was temporarily housed. These changes are often unanticipated and seldom fully fathomed by the person experiencing them. But they are real nonetheless.

—Philip Jackson

INTRODUCTION

Teachers tend to remember their failures most vividly and tend to never truly know their long-term influence, but there are times when the evidence is mostly incontrovertible: we have had undeniable successes. Sometimes these are specific and particular accomplishments; other times they are related directly to our ongoing duty to be a safety net for our students. My first group of stories is about probable successes with students; the second group is about how teachers act as safety nets; and the last group is about a different kind of success teachers too rarely experience.

PROBABLE SUCCESS

In truth, I've only reluctantly included the following examples of probable success. There are two very good reasons teachers are reluctant to
crow about their successes. First, if there is a success, we know that we
are only one of many influences that helped bring it about and we would
not want to detract from the student's responsibility for that success. Second, we acutely realize that "success" with a student is a tentative success,
and may not last.

Will

Ironically, the most important results I seem to have had appear to have
nothing to do with how I taught my subject, which is not to say I do not
highly value teaching my subject. Students making important academic
progress were often not responding so much to my teaching as responding to me. (I am not, repeat *not*, negating the importance of literacy and
good teaching, but there are other important values that we must also provide as teachers.) The first week of school, when I had not yet gotten
bogged down in teacher's duties, I went to visit one of my students, Will
Fernandez, in the hospital. He had been in a severe car accident. I even
took him some work to do in the hospital. He appreciated my effort, if not
the work.

Will was cool about the visit; he never mentioned it once back at
school. But Will was doing A work. Will had never had an A before. I had
a distinct feeling that the A-caliber work he was doing in my class (as
compared to any other work he had ever done before) was not because I
was such an effective classroom teacher. Our apparent success as teachers
is often determined by how our students react to us simply as people.

Jose

Probably my greatest single success in my first year of teaching had nothing to do directly with my class, my curriculum, or my personal efforts.
Jose Gardena, a quiet, soft-spoken, very intelligent student, stuttered
badly. He wanted to do something about it and asked me to help. Totally
untrained in speech, I tried to help for a little while. I even gave him my

portable tape recorder to use to practice. But I realized very quickly I could not handle the problem.

Jose had tried to see the school district's speech therapist before, but it hadn't happened. Jose probably did not push hard enough. I was determined the speech therapist would see him. He did. Within two months after he started seeing the speech therapist, Jose had quit stuttering. One of the warmest moments I have experienced came near the end of that third quarter. I pulled a Wordsworth/Coleridge assignment on the class. (Did you know the *Rhyme of the Ancient Mariner* was written as an untrue story told as true? Wordsworth and Coleridge—at least I was told this in college—had a contest to see who could write the best piece of literature. Coleridge was to write an unbelievable tale as true, and Wordsworth the opposite.) Jose's class had the option of either fabricating a story and making it sound believable, or telling a true story but making it sound a lie. The class members then tried to determine whether the storyteller was lying or not.

Jose told an incredible, but realistic story about when he lived in Arizona. He had been hunting with his brother when they became separated. In the story a mountain lion jumped him and knocked him down. The mountain lion was scared, not angry, and ran. But Jose was hurt and his brother had to carry him to help. The class intently discussed whether Jose had lied; they concurred Jose had told the truth. Jose announced he had lied. He received a most spontaneous and most warm ovation. Not only had he quit stuttering, he had become an effective speaker. And I hadn't taught him a thing. I had just insured he had an opportunity to see the speech therapist he was entitled to see anyway.

For teachers success comes in many forms.

Rebecca

Another very bright student was Rebecca. She was identified as Chicana and was in "dumbbell" (C-track) English—which probably seemed appropriate since she had never done better than D work in English. The only irony was that she was as smart as any of the kids in my advanced English class (yes, even "academically" as smart). Occasionally I gave the same tests to all levels of my English classes. As Herndon (1971, p. 85) points out, schools usually do an effective job of separating the sheep and the goats. Only Rebecca got the fourth-highest score among all of my students on a test (analyzed to be both valid and reliable), and she did not cheat. Rebecca's "problem" was her peer group. She did not want to appear smarter than any of her friends and her friends always got Ds in English. Fortunately, her friends did not happen to be in my English class. Given that break, she did very well and I transferred her to my advanced class. She didn't do any better there, but then she did not do any worse, just A-caliber work. It was probably an imposition of my values to transfer her, but she didn't seem to mind that someone had finally discovered what she could really do.

It is the exception, but teachers are invariably talent scouts and often have noted successes with diamonds in the rough.

Bob

The school nearly lost Bob. He was really dropping out, at first psychologically, and then physically. Bob only had to show up to graduate, but he even stopped showing up. I was really concerned about him. So I started a "Keep Bob in School" campaign. I sent notices to all his friends. The notice said, "When you see Bob, ask him one of three questions: Did you do your assignments today? Did you make first-period class? Are you going to graduate?"

Bob was rather amazed at all the attention, so I put it to him straight: "Do you want to graduate?" Naturally he said yes. So I really put it to him. "I don't mean do you just want to, will you?"

"Yes," he said.

"Good, I'll see you at five thirty tomorrow morning. I'll pick you up for class."

"Five thirty?"

"Five thirty!"

At five thirty, I dragged him out of bed and into school for the next couple of weeks. Bob caught up with his work in the quiet morning hours, and then I relied on him to stick with it. He waited until seven thirty to come to school thereafter, but he stuck to his studies and graduated. A couple of years later, he told me he nearly cried when I offered to pick him up. And I was worried he might think I was overstepping my bounds.

A teacher cannot do this for every student, but we can make a difference in specific cases.

TEACHERS AS A SAFETY NET

A teacher tries to protect each student in the classroom from bullies, from humiliation, from her- or himself. A teacher also tries to organize a variety of activities so that each student has some success, and each student has to struggle with his or her comfort level. Loving sports, I especially enjoyed teaching physical education. I of course love football, basketball, and baseball, but also kickball, wall ball, and four square, as well as obstacle courses, mini-Olympics, and sports from other cultures. This was an elementary school experience.

I appreciated that I often had girls who were as good all-around athletes as some of the boys. I especially enjoyed when a playoff was between a girl and a boy. I had one particularly good athlete, Esteban, who was also a really nice kid and a good student academically. He seemingly did everything well athletically. No matter what we did in P.E. class, Esteban was the best.

There was another boy in this class, Lance, who was invariably the worst in class—again, no matter what we did. All year long I hadn't found anything Lance could do. And despite all my efforts, it was very difficult to keep him from being the class scapegoat.

Then one day Esteban, the most popular kid in class, decided we should all go bowling. I rather hated the idea. I didn't want to spend class time that way, but because it was Esteban, the whole class was behind him. I agreed, although it was mostly an after-school activity.

Parents drove. We arrived at the bowling alley. Ah (or ugh)—that smell bowling alleys have. I think it's the rental shoes. Ah, the lanes, the excited nine-year-olds, who for the most part had to use both hands to lift the ball. The nine-year-olds who tended to drop the ball on the lanes more than roll them. And the gutter balls. What an enjoyable time. Esteban was outshining the others, rolling a 100 the first time he'd ever bowled. He was outshining all others except Lance—who shot something like a 187. Who'd have guessed? Esteban was impressed with Lance. The class was impressed with Lance. It was entirely different for Lance in the class from that moment onward.

Esteban thought to go bowling, not me. But as a teacher I reaped the benefit. Lance reaped the benefit. A teacher is always a part of something much bigger. Success is where you find it.

Ron

Another problem among teachers is that you are asked for advice so often, you can start giving it indiscriminately. Ron Encarnacion was a student assistant for another teacher and we often talked during my free period. We had something in common: we had both lived on Guam. Due to a number of home pressures, Ron had decided to join the army before school was out. Some teachers told Ron he was crazy. That's all, just "he was crazy." They didn't think to ask him what his rationale was, how firm a decision it was, or what his alternatives were, they just told him he was crazy.

Most of the students at our high school who decided to join the service probably were crazy, trying to run away from one set of problems into another set. But that was not the case with Ron. Ron had thought it out and was determined. All the people telling him he was crazy just made him feel bad. I would never advise anyone specifically to join the army or any other organization, but I encouraged Ron. Before he left he thanked me as the only one who gave him any moral support. Ron's still in the service; he's married, has a kid, and is doing fine.

Sometimes getting out of the way is the key to success.

Ike

I considered Ike Kerner a discovery. Ike had never done very well in school, at least to hear him tell it, and the reason was that he couldn't spell. Writing skills are the chief means by which a student is evaluated in schools, just as reading is the chief way in which kids are expected to learn. At that time, I had given little or no thought to any form of evaluation other than writing except an occasional oral report. That was the way things were. What I had discovered was that a student who answered a question without making any spelling mistakes, and got some of the punctuation right, was more likely to get a better grade than the student who had fine ideas and miserable spelling.

Ike's spelling was atrocious, but his ideas were good. He might spell "pilot" "ploit," but at least he got the right letters in there (in Ike's case, it did not turn out to be a perceptual problem, he just couldn't spell). I made a value judgment that spelling alone should not keep Ike from getting an A and gave him an A despite the spelling errors. That seemed an important concession on my part at the time. I still recognize the importance of good spelling and that people judge others by such factors as spelling, but I have also met some very bright people who are very successful who spell horribly. So it's certainly not the *only* criteria for success, even in a high school English class.

Once in class I was able to do Ike a favor. Ike was a tall gangly kid who was a bit awkward, physically and socially. He was an excellent football player, but because he could make a blunder now and then, his excellence in sports was largely overlooked. In an important league game against Dane Thicke High School, Fields was down by six points late in the game. Ike played rushing tackle so he really showed something to me when he nearly caught a halfback from behind who had beaten Fields' defensive backs and was running downfield for an apparent touchdown. I would not have guessed he was that fast.

Ike was quick and, late in this game, he showed his speed again. He got into Thicke's backfield so fast he actually took a handoff meant for their team's halfback. Terrific, except poor, unfortunate Ike ran the wrong way. Fortunately one of his own men tackled him immediately and Fields still had a chance to win the game, with the good field position Ike had provided. But Fields did not move the ball and lost. Ike was the goat. He could have scored a touchdown if he had run the right way. The next day in class someone was razzing him from behind, calling him "Wrong Way Kerner." It had been funny to see, but I knew Ike's laughing response to the other students' joking was strained.

"Did you know some guys in the pros have run the wrong way? It even happened at a Rose Bowl game. Seriously. I've seen film clips of it. Players picked up fumbles and went all the way for what they thought were touchdowns. I remember a guy on my basketball team shot at the wrong basket a couple of times. Fortunately he wasn't too good. Missed both times. Another thing I noticed in that Thicke game was that if any of our defensive backs had hustled after that Thicke back like Ike did, Thicke wouldn't have scored their first touchdown. And if Ike hadn't picked off that handoff, you guys wouldn't have had another easy chance to score," I commented.

The other players in the class of course couldn't argue with a teacher lecture. Regardless, I think it took some heat off Ike and at least they didn't call him "Wrong Way" in my class thereafter. An often overlooked, but vital function of teaching is to protect students and allow them room to make mistakes and grow because of their mistakes. Students' peer groups can be unmerciful.

Theodore

Theodore would have been my candidate for least likely to graduate in four years. For one thing, his family's lifestyle was not real stable. When I had Theodore in class, he was living with his parents in a recreational vehicle parked near the school. They had sold their house and had moved out on the street. Theodore asked me over one day, and I could understand why he did not spend too much time at home. I met his mother who was friendly, but the place was too small. Theodore was nonetheless pretty excited about driving the thing around and their built-in stereo and TV. After I had visited Theodore he turned in his all-time first writing assignment. I was exceedingly happy Theodore had decided to trust me enough to write something. I hope you can appreciate that he had something to say: "I feel unhappy when you like someone very much and they start taking drugs and stealing stuff from other people and they start cutting school. And than they get caught and get send up to Juvenile Hall for a couple of days and than comes home and won't do no work for their mother and then they do it all over again and the police come out and picks them up and takes them to Juvenile Hall and then they send them to the ranch for about a couple of years."

The main reason I didn't figure Theodore would graduate, however, was not his severe grammar (and reading) problems, but that he seldom came to school. Theodore had a redeeming quality, though, that pulled him through. He was easygoing and very likeable. He was always in trouble, but he always took it good-naturedly. That's how it seems to work: the kids that take all the flak get to hang around. Theodore took the flak and somehow during the next three years he put it all together, learned to read, and did enough assignments to pass enough classes to graduate.

Did I help him? Yes. Did I make a difference? Who knows? But I know personally that any help you get along the way is much appreciated.

Ennis

Ennis Dowd was another kid I really respected. Ennis took longer to learn things than most kids did, so he was relegated to getting poor grades in most classes. It wasn't because he couldn't do the work, but because he couldn't keep up with the pace. (During a fire cracker epidemic at school, Ennis was the only person to be suspended. He was the only one ever caught lighting a firecracker. It was probably the only one he had ever lit, but it would never have occurred to Ennis to be sneaky.) But Ennis was a reader, an avid reader; he loved to read and read more books than any other student in my classes.

Besides finding books for Ennis to read, I also discovered Ennis as an athletic team manager. It's a thankless but important job on any high school team. Ennis asked to be my team's manager and he did such a fantastic job of keeping up with all our gear and records, he was recruited as manager for both varsity baseball and varsity football the following year. Ennis was a great kid, but the kind of person seldom appreciated in a system that traditionally rewards only scholars and athletes.

I always felt like I'd discovered Ennis even though he'd always been there.

HASSLES WITH PARENTS

I want to end this chapter with two otherwise peripheral successes, both of which are related to my role as a teacher-educator and neither of which are about my own relationship to one of my own students.

I am hopeful that the non-teacher who reads this book will get a sense from the early examples of the kind of successes that are the stuff of teaching, while realizing that teachers want to give at least most of the credit to the student. I suspect teachers are more likely to appreciate the following two stories, because our sense of unqualified success is really generally limited to the petty battles that so frequently litter our days. Maybe you have to be a teacher (or an administrator) to appreciate the degree of my pride in triumphing over haughty parents.

Mr. Paine

One hectic spring day, my attendance clerk came in to tell me a student had stolen attendance cards that were used to report student absences from a seventh-period class, the last class of the day. I was particularly keen on catching the perpetrators in this kind of theft to insure that such rare occurrences stayed rare occurrences. I rushed over to the classroom and asked if any students would testify as to whom had taken the cards. Ordinarily, I would call students out of class one by one so no one else in the class could know who "squealed," but in this case five students quickly raised their hands. They said it had been Nan Paine and that she had done it to protect a friend who was cutting that class that period. I checked and Nan was out of her own class. I looked for her on campus and couldn't find her. I called her mother at home.

"Mrs. Paine. Is Nan there?" I asked.

"No. She should be at school," Nan's mother replied.

"Well, she's not. At least not in class."

"Uh oh! "

"Mrs. Paine, I have witnesses who say they saw Nan steal some of our attendance cards."

"Why would she do a thing like that?" she asked.

"Ordinarily to keep a friend from being turned in absent so they won't get caught cutting," I explained.

"Oh. Are you sure it was Nan?"

"I have several witnesses who clearly recognized her."

"Well, what happens now?"

"I want to hear Nan's side of it, but assuming she did it, she is suspended two days and I would like a parent conference, if possible, before her return."

"Well. I'll try to find Nan and get back to you."

"Good. She will be welcome back Friday, unless there's some new information."

The next morning at 7:50 a.m., Mr. Paine and Nan were at school expecting an immediate appointment. I don't personally believe in stopping what I am doing for the convenience of someone who had apparently screwed up, so I finished my work in the attendance office. I helped students get admitted to class on time by 8:00 and went over and met Mr. Paine and Nan at 8:05.

"Mr. Paine. This is Dr. Gose." My secretary introduced me to Nan's father. I always appreciated how Ophelia said "Dr." Gose when she was expecting I might have trouble with a parent.

"Hello. Glad to meet you. Hello Nan. Won't you both come into my office?"

We went into my office and sat around my round table (which I had bartered with our librarian for). It was most evident from his agitated state that Mr. Paine was looking for some kind of vindication. His daughter Nan, who had large Betty Boop eyes (do you remember the cartoon?), had a plaintive expressive on her face. Mr. Paine looked like he was in a traffic jam on the way to work and seemed very irate he had to come in on his own time to right a wrong.

"I want to know why you suspended my daughter." Well, he certainly got to the point in a hurry.

"As I told your wife, witnesses said she stole attendance cards. Nan was cutting her last period so I couldn't get her side of the story, so pending any new information, she was suspended two days."

"Nan, you cut seventh period yesterday?" Mr. Paine asked Nan.

"Well, yes."

"Where did you go?"

"Well, just around."

"Well, never mind. We'll talk about that when we get home." He turned to me. "The point is, she didn't take the cards."

"Mr. Paine, five witnesses say positively that she did," I said.

"And I want to find out why they lied about my daughter. She has a witness who can verify Nan was somewhere else. What's her name, Nan? Oh yeah, Katie Stroh?"

"Let me go find Katie Stroh and see the other witnesses again, too," I said. I spent the next twenty minutes out on campus running down the witnesses. All five of my witnesses were outstanding students; they weren't friends of each other; they had no apparent antagonisms toward Nan; and they were absolutely positive Nan had taken the cards. Katie Stroh was cutting P.E. and therefore unavailable. I went back to the Paines with this information.

"Mr. Paine, I find it really difficult not to believe the witnesses."

"Look, what's going on around here? What's the matter with this school anyway? I think you just made a mistake and are trying to cover it up." He showed restraint but was clearly seething. There was hostility in his words.

"Mr. Paine, let me spend some more time on this. I can only judge by the information that I have and I'd like to find Nan's witness. But I need to tell you I've never been in a situation this clear in which the person in your daughter's position hasn't been lying." I had put myself on the spot. Now I had to prove it one way or the other. I had taken a stand.

"Fine! Find her then! You'll see," he said threateningly.

I spent another half an hour or more double-checking with a couple of the witnesses. They said they would even testify in court if somehow it came to that. And then I finally found Katie Stroh on the back side of campus. The principal was out of his office, so I used his office to implement my normal strategy of separating "criminals" for questioning. I grilled Katie for about forty-five minutes. For forty-four minutes she corroborated Nan's story. She was almost convincing, but it just didn't add up that the other witnesses were all mistaken and that Nan had been with Katie instead of busy stealing the cards. But Katie insisted they both had been cutting class and couldn't have been there to steal the cards, that the other witnesses were lying or saw someone else who looked like Nan, and that, besides, the witnesses didn't like Nan.

Her story was almost believable, but I went for broke. "Katie, I hear what you're saying and I have to either believe you and Nan or the others. I'm sorry, but I believe the others. They were in class and seem to be more credible witnesses. This may go to court because of the suspension, so I'm going to call the police and have them take an affidavit from you. If this goes to court and you're wrong, I want it clear that it is your perjury. With that I'll take my chances." I was bluffing.

"Wow, you really do things differently around here. They weren't so strict where I came from. I didn't think it was such a big deal. Nan called me last night and asked me to tell this story. Wow. I don't want to sign any paper."

"You won't have to. You can go. Thank you for at least finally telling the truth." I suppose I should have thought of some disciplinary measure for the trouble Katie had caused, but I figured her dealing with Nan, or even Nan's father, might be enough. I went back to the Paines, my pace quickened and suppressing a grin. I reentered my office abruptly. Mr. Paine was hunched over the table, very self-contained, frowning. I think he was ready to let me have it for having been gone so long.

"Nan, your witness cracked. She says you lied."

"What?" Mr. Paine exclaimed. Nan squirmed in her seat.

"Her witness says she lied," I repeated.

"Is that true, Nan?" her father asked.

"Well, yes." Nan admitted.

"How could you do this to me?" Mr. Paine asked his daughter.

"Well, I . . ."

"I'm taking you home."

"Thanks for coming in, Mr. Paine," I said. And I said no more. I didn't chastise Nan. I didn't complain to Mr. Paine about the two hours this fiasco had taken. I had taken all the necessary precautions. I was Sherlock Holmes. I had solved the case. The father had treated me contemptuously, even rudely. I had been polite, if to the point. Then I won. Schools reflect society's competitive social structure. Philosophically I don't like having to have winners and losers. But pushed into a corner, I like to win. Such is the stuff of school administration.

Mrs. Butz

Who is rude: the person who refuses to be interrupted or the person who allows interruptions? Who is more righteous: the person who allows kooks to dominate their agendas or the person who sanctions the kooks? You pay a price either way.

Mrs. Butz took up incredible time from teachers, administrators, and staff in our district. She was a full-blown, bona fide "kook" trying to impress others with her importance. She was rude, unreasonable, demanding, and offensive. She demanded constant attention and was extremely successful in achieving that goal. What baffles me is that people reinforced her self-importance by catering to it. *Pas moi.* I did not look for a confrontation, but neither did I avoid it when it finally came—even if she did sneak up on me.

The day she did approach me I was talking discreetly to a teacher in an isolated area of a classroom hallway on a confidential matter about personnel. (We were being discrete because I was about to hire a staff member away from another program in the district since she and her boss were at an apparently irreparable breach.) Mrs. Butz came up from my blind side, interrupted Rob Bing, to whom I was speaking. She demanded immediate help. With some surprise that she would be down at that end of campus, I went ahead and told her I was discussing a confidential matter with Mr. Bing and that I would be right with her. As Mr. Bing started his next sentence, she interrupted again. You may surmise she was surprised by my response.

"Mrs. Butz, you're being very rude. I'll be with you as soon as Mr. Bing is finished." I told her firmly, but in no way antagonistically.

"Well, I never," she said. Then her last words were that she would see the superintendent. Oh well. So it gose.

About twelve to fifteen minutes later, I saw her in the attendance office. I asked her if she still needed help. She informed me she was under the directive of the superintendent not to talk to me. Perfect. I never did have to talk to her again. But I watched bemusedly as countless others spent hours and hours trying to reason with her. They were in fact catering to her, reinforcing her very negative, destructive behavior. Some time later, while I was clearly in good favor, I half seriously proposed to the district's administrative cabinet that it would be less expensive to have a full-time administrator assigned directly to Mrs. Butz.

Although I believe I handled this matter as it should have been handled by all administrators, it was with some liability. She of course complained about me to each of my supervisors and to each school board member in turn. Although each of these persons must have known what kind of problem Mrs. Butz posed, and must have tired of her threatening legal action, they also didn't like hearing about her conflict with me; I suspect many of my superiors were annoyed that I hadn't protected them by giving her whatever she wanted regardless of the consequences. By the time everyone was fed up with her and couldn't care less if she went ahead and sued, no one seemed to think about how they could have kept her from obtaining such a full head of steam by having confronted her much earlier. It would have been better not to make so many concessions to her, raising her expectations of attention so high. Once more my name was associated with that albatross "controversy." Controversy is the bane of promotions. But not ever having to talk to that virago was worth any professional consequences. The story of our encounter was told repeatedly to the delight of the rest of the faculty and staff; and I enjoyed even hearing others tell of my legendary bout with the Butz.

It's not what someone outside of teaching might think of as a major success, but most teachers will love the luck I had in dealing with an unreasonable parent. We don't get many satisfying stories about such encounters.

I May Only Be a Teacher, But I Am a Teacher

Schools provide the venue for teachers to be one of the last safety nets to catch everything from behavioral and emotional problems to medical, eyesight, and other physical problems.

—Janice Gose

These are the people [to whom] we've entrusted our children, who we say are so important. And they [teachers] accept that charge with inadequate support and modest pay.

—Janice Gose

If I had a child who wanted to be a teacher, I would bid him Godspeed as if he were going to a war. For indeed the war against prejudice, greed, and ignorance is eternal, and those who dedicate themselves to it give their lives no less because they may live to see some fraction of the battle won.

—James Hilton

A teacher affects eternity; he can never tell where his influence stops.

—Henry Adams

I met James about four years after he left my class. He had just finished his junior year at a high school in the Bronx and was all-city honorable mention in basketball. James was friendly for the first time since I'd known him, though his fists and jaws were no more relaxed than they were in the sixth grade. He told me he had loved to watch me try to teach him, that it was a battle of wills and he had been determined to win. But he also told me that he had listened even though he never responded to me and that he had taught himself to read and write well enough to stay in high school and play ball. He also thanked me for not throwing him out of class.

—Herbert Kohl

The necessary rule a teacher has is to protect students against themselves.

—Jim McGoldrick

I may only be a teacher, but I *am* a teacher! I first read a quotation to that effect in one of the books on teaching from the 1960s, perhaps it was by Jonathon Kozol. After having taught for two years, I was very frustrated by the problems I had in the classroom that were beyond my control. I tried social work and the ministry and returned to teaching with the knowledge that for me, teaching gave more leverage in working with people than I had fully appreciated. The stories in this chapter are not about successes or failures, but are meant to be a testimony to how teachers are often invested in "process," because they are simply not in a position to overcome some obstacles and change results. They are, nonetheless, there as teachers to provide a human touch and a positive influence regardless of outcomes.

I would argue that some of my very best work was done with the following nine students, yet perhaps to no long-term lasting effect. All the rhetoric about goals and measurable results has its place in education. But what it means to be a teacher is more deeply invested in the human relationships we have with students, which may not have any measurable results.

The most ironic case I remember of a situation you wished you could change was that of a girl whose father kicked her off the roof for being slow in handing him the Christmas lights he was putting up. It might have sounded almost accidental on his part except he had earlier hit her in the head with a rifle butt. But these really aren't situations a teacher can do much about, even if it is in his or her job description. All a teacher can help a student to do is to try to assume responsibility to do something about his or her own situation.

NINE LIVES

Here are the stories of nine students who touched my life in some incalculable way. I may only be a teacher, but I am a teacher.

Bessie

If I could have taught all my students just one thing in every one of my class, it would be that each person has countless good reasons why she or he would fail, and that if she or he uses those reasons she or he will fail. Bessie took those words seriously. She lived at home with her mother and three younger siblings. Her father, who no longer lived there, would sometimes get drunk, go over to the house, and beat the younger children. That was Bessie's predicament. What she wanted was a situation where the beatings could not happen. How do you get there? she wanted to know.

She talked to her mother about the situation; she could not talk to her father. One of the things I learned that year was that county agencies can sometimes be helpful. I put Bessie in contact with a child protection agency. Her mother was not real pleased to hear from a social worker, and shunned the social worker. But Bessie had not failed. Her mother really did have the resources to keep her father out of the house, and realizing how serious Bessie was, she did keep the father away. I discovered very often that people can do things they say they cannot.

Mack

Mack Bronson sat in my class all year. Occasionally, he would do something absolutely brilliant. For the most part, though, he came to class, did none of the assignments, passed none of the tests, and said nothing in class. About twice a month I would go to him personally, ask him if he wanted some alternative assignments, ask him if he hated the class, ask him if there was some other teacher he thought he might do better with, if there was anything I could do to be a better teacher for him. To each question he gave a polite, "No." He also said that I was his favorite teacher. It was just a personal statement to his parents that he was determined to fail all of his classes.

Doug and Jenny

Who is more noteworthy? A student who had never previously read more than one or two books a year who reads twenty-three books in one semester, or a student who had never read a book at all who reads and enjoys her first? Both students are memorable to me. The former was eighteen and could have dropped out of school legally, except he wanted to graduate. He had had polio as a child and depended on a metal shaft in the femur of his left leg. He had an operation yearly; after his operation that year, he carried the old metal shaft they'd taken out of his leg around with him as a conversation piece. And he still insisted on playing basketball when we played.

Doug had an interesting attitude toward his malady. He ignored it. He refused to not play basketball. He preferred half court, but he'd even play full court. He would not permit himself to be limited. He'd rather take his chances and go ahead and have to have an operation each year. (After all," he said, "the state of California [Medi-Cal] paid for them.") Doug read the twenty-three books that year.

Jenny read the one book, and that book was *Catcher in the Rye*. Jenny was a reasonably attractive teenager. "Sexy" would probably be a word she'd like to hear used to describe her. She had a foul mouth and occasionally ran away from home for careless reasons. I was codirecting a small, experimental, public high school program and this was Jenny's first successful schooling experience. Not only did she read her first book, but she was succeeding as a teacher's aide at the elementary school. Despite Jenny's newfound success, we got in trouble with her mom.

I think we can assume Jenny left her book, *Catcher in the Rye,* lying around the house so her mother would ask about it. I don't know whether she wanted her mom to find out she'd read a book, or be shocked that Jenny was reading a book that had many years before been banned in Boston.

Her mom called us, although she didn't want Jenny to know she had. I took the call.

"Hi. This is Mrs. Davies. Jenny's mom."

"Good morning, Mrs. Davies," I answered pleasantly enough.

Somehow, I naïvely thought she had probably called to thank us because (a) Jenny was going to school full-time; (b) Jenny was reading her first book; (c) Jenny was not running away since school started; or (d) some other thing. It was clearly "other."

"I wanted to ask you about a book Jenny's been reading."

"Sure," I answered helpfully. "Which one does she have?"

"*Catcher in the Rye.*"

"Oh."

"Did you assign that book?"

"No m'am, although it probably is a book she got from the bookcase here."

"Do you think kids should read that sort of stuff?"

"Mrs. Davies, I know the book used to be controversial. But that was a long time ago. Most English teachers consider it a classic now. It's approved by virtually every library now."

"But don't you think the kids pick up that kind of language by reading it?"

Did she not know of her daughter's foul mouth before she had read the book? I wondered.

"Mrs. Davies. I kind of wish it were that easy. If it were, our kids would speak more grammatical English because of all they listen to on TV."

"I'd never really thought about that."

"Well, I agree with you Mrs. Davies that the language isn't particularly appropriate for teenagers to use, but it is a worthy story."

"Well . . ."

"Mrs. Davies, I think the key point to note right now is how well Jenny has been doing in school. I'm too proud of her for reading her first book to fuss at her too much for her selection. She's been doing such a super job."

Thus, through diplomacy, we averted a possible controversy that in our school district could have been a huge disaster. And Jenny, for an extended time, continued to do well in the program (until she finally ran away from home again).

Ben

As far as we know, Ben was the only bona fide "failure" we had in our program, the same program Jenny had been in. We only accepted Ben into our experimental program because we were single-mindedly committed to taking anyone who asked to come. I had known Ben from an earlier school year at the school that sponsored our program.

Ben was, at least during that time, the most useless human being I had ever come across. He spoiled most (I'd say all) of my theories about human nature. He was a classic user in every sense, but especially of drugs and people.

With us, he had the three best weeks he'd probably ever had in school since seventh grade, but Bart, the codirector, and I were never fooled. We never knew why he chose to come to our program, though we had feared he would. We had observed him the year before. He was infamous for having turned narc on some drug "friends" to get himself out of jail. His decision to enroll in our program may have been related to that. I think it more likely that he had already developed a lust for one of our other students, Ronnie.

Ronnie was the mother of our group. She looked out for the well-being of each of our students. Ronnie'd call when the students were suspiciously late; clean up the coffee mess when Bart and I were fed up with it; talk and laugh to keep everyone comfortable. She was also a missionary. And Ben Hoss became her crusade.

To Ronnie's credit, she leveled with Ben from the start that she was not interested in him as a boyfriend. To our credit, we never let Ronnie think we thought she was being helpful. And later telling her "I told you so" wasn't comforting or necessary.

For the three weeks Ben thought he had a chance with Ronnie, he was a model student: no drugs, prompt attendance, successful participation. When he saw that his affection was not reciprocated, he found he could still get Ronnie's quick attention by falling back into drug use.

I suppose it's a classic pattern between the "outlaw" and the "nice girl" with the misguided maternal instincts. Ronnie didn't rehabilitate him.

My, what a hassle he was. His mom, taking stock of Ben's three good weeks, started thinking we had been a miracle cure. She wouldn't publicly admit to anything less. So when he started screwing up again, she asked what we had done to cause it. She couldn't complain about a lack of attention though. We even went to the house and literally dragged him from his Oscarlike (*The Odd Couple*) unkempt bedroom to school.

When Ronnie finally gave up on Ben, after an interminable series of long, deep (boring) conversations, Ben quit coming to school. He said he was going to commit suicide, which seemed unlikely. He did make one final plea for help, admitting to me he was indeed a heroin addict and needed help. I spent the day with Ben at a free clinic and then, in snarled L. A. freeway commuter traffic, I brought him back, but he never followed up with the program the clinic recommended.

This experience had no redeeming social value. We wasted a lot of valuable human resources being manipulated by Ben. Bart and I at least minimized the expense, feeling clearly that investments should be made on students solving, not creating, problems. I have no hope that anything good ever came of our relationship with Ben. After that I no longer believed that all problems were solvable. Ben was not a victim of our "self-fulfilling" prophecy. Ben was not a victim. Ben was deliberate and capable of choosing his particular experience of life.

I may only be a teacher, but I am a teacher. I am glad that we were there to fail, responsibly, with Ben.

Two Vandals

Two vandals caused damage valued at $40,000 or more at Fontara High School where I worked as vice principal. I discovered it at 7:00 one morning when I had gotten to work early in the vain thought I would catch up on some work. Our local police were able to solve the case. The boys—former students who had been sent to a continuation school (only one of them had attended the school even briefly)—had left their fingerprints all over the place. As is the case with most successful arrests, they must have wanted to get caught. When we found out who had done the damage, my feelings of frustration turned more toward futility. I felt more sad than angry.

I had reason to believe that a year before, one of these boys had abandoned a friend, one of our other students, who had passed out from sniffing glue and died before he was found. This boy, who I suspect fled, lived in a mobile home with an alcoholic grandmother who died while he was still in custody for the vandalism. His mother had died when he was an infant. His father had abandoned him. When the boy was released on probation from the vandalism case, he could not return to school, but he did go back to the mobile home to live by himself. I felt so helpless. It's not easy accepting the reality that I may only be a teacher, but that I am a teacher.

J.D.

The most pathetic and tragic episode I have ever witnessed happened at Panorama High School. I had a limited role as a reading and English teacher there. We had at the school a student who matched textbook descriptions of schizophrenia. J.D. came to class each day, sat down, opened his book, and looked at the same page until the class ended. After four months, the only thing he had ever said to anyone was "don't touch me," which he had said a total of three times. I was just as happy he was not in my classroom. For all my idealism, I was never a crusader. But his situation got to me just the same. An incident that happened to J.D. caused me inescapable despondence.

One afternoon at school, we really messed things up for J.D. We let the other students out early without ringing the school bell. We were supposed to have a faculty meeting. J.D. just stayed in his seat. It was raining outside and getting cold and the doors were opening a lot and J.D. did not have on any warm clothes. I guess he started feeling a bit strange about all the attention he was starting to receive from the teachers in the room and he started shivering a little. That freaked out one of the teachers who started making unnecessary commotion, asking "What do we do?" Things got worse suddenly when the school secretary rang the school bell for some unknown reason—habit, I suppose. J.D. heard the bell, his usual signal, and got up to leave. By this time, everyone was worried J.D. was having some sort of breakdown and someone had called his mother, who was unfortunately not at home. Meanwhile, he started walking for the rearmost of the two exits for the building. The principal ran to head him off. J.D. turned when he reached the principal's upheld hands and walked back toward the front exit, whereupon the vice principal ran and blocked that exit with his ample girth. For the next few minutes J.D. walked from exit to exit only to be rebuffed; like a mechanical robot, he would turn and walk back toward the other exit. The principal's secretary called the fire department—sure, why not the fire department? It was clear no one at school knew what to do. The principal realized he was expected to do something, after all he was principal, so he tried to put his arm around J.D.'s shoulder. Seeing as how the only thing J.D. had ever said was, "don't touch me," I had to figure that wasn't a real good idea. Sure enough, J.D. spoke for the fourth time that year. "Don't touch me," he said. The principal quickly obliged and J.D. continued to walk from door to door. A fireman finally came in the front entrance; he, of course, didn't know what to do. However, thank God, right behind him came J.D.'s mother. She told us she had been parked out in front all this time. The principal, vice principal, and mother all thought this funny and laughed. I knew it was ironic, but it certainly was not funny enough to laugh about. She took J.D. directly home. I had thought he would finally be taken to a doctor, but no, he only went home.

While I was trying to take all this in, the very next words from our fearless leader, the principal, were, "Well, let's get on with the faculty meeting." As soon as we were seated, his very next words were, "What do you think about the new furniture we want to order?" I was horrified, but didn't know what to do. Obviously no one knew what to do, so we pretended nothing had happened, just as we did my first year of teaching when we confronted the drug problem and riot. Our faculty meeting continued as if there had been no incident.

I took a three-hour drive to my very favorite restaurant. I didn't figure anything out, but I did come back to school the next day and request to have J.D. assigned to my class when, and if, he came back. He came back to school a week or so later and he was put into my class. I had been reading Glasser's *Reality Therapy* so I decided to try my understanding of Glasser's approach. I decided to treat J.D. just like all my other students, including holding him to the same expectations. Each day when the students came into my class, I asked each student individually what he or she intended to do that day; I told them if they wrote their goals down, they should get credit for them. Each day, when J.D. came into the room I talked to him in his turn, put the assignment sheet in front of him, and left him the same choice the other students had, whether to do it or not. For two weeks he came into my class, opened his book to the same page, and apparently ignored me when I talked to him. But I did it every day regardless. During the third week something happened to make me think I must be the greatest teacher in the whole world. Like every other day, I went to J.D., in his turn, gave him the assignment sheet, and explained his alternatives. I always looked him in the eyes, although he always looked only at his book. On an otherwise unnoteworthy Wednesday, J.D. took the sheet, looked up at me, and said, "Thank you." J.D. had talked for the fifth time and it was the first time he had said anything other than "don't touch me."

I was elated, but since that was obviously all he wanted to tell me, I left it at that with my own simple thank you. I envisioned great things, and was awfully impressed with myself. But it was the last time J.D. spoke at school and a few weeks later he left for good. We were told he was finally getting professional help, but that may have been wishful thinking on our part.

I am more Glasserian than Freudian, if that means I am more concerned with changing behavior in the present than figuring out what caused it in the past, but I did some research to find out why J.D. might have been the way he was. This is what I discovered:

It seems J.D. was once a good B student, and a good athlete besides. And he was really a straight, quiet kid. He went to a school, however, that had a number of "dopers" and the high school administration was cracking down on them. Unfortunately, J.D. made the mistake of having some sort of seizure during school time (from the description it sounds like he had an epileptic fit). The hard-nosed vice principal assumed it was a reaction to drugs and without any kind of due process, busted J.D. on a drug rap and suspended him. J.D. was sent to the continuation school effective when his suspension was over. Apparently J.D. tried to argue for himself, but was shouted down. The intimidation, the possible epilepsy, and a pending divorce at home left J.D. with minimal resistance. Trying to explain himself to that vice principal was the last time J.D. talked in school other than to say "don't touch me," and once, "thank you."

I remind myself, I may only be a teacher, but I am a teacher.

EXTRA: BAD ADVICE

The most commonly related bad advice given in school:

1. You should always do your best work. Nonsense: save your best for what's most important.
2. You already need to know what you need to do in life. Rubbish: Most people change careers at least three times.
3. Grades are incredibly important. Balderdash: grades predict future grades, but grades for students within the same class do not predict world success.

4. Avoid the subjects you are bad at. Ridiculous: you might be the next Bob Dylan, and who would want to miss out on art and music regardless of apparent talent?
5. Enroll in your favorite subjects. Wrong: take the best teachers almost without regard to what they teach.
6. Don't rock the boat and make waves. Misguided: you only find out how the system works by causing exceptions.
7. Patience is a virtue. Not likely.
8. Do what you are told. Highly unlikely
9. Act your age. This would be a disaster. No child is genetically and/or biologically programmed to stay in his or her seat six hours a day.

6

The Curriculum

Teaching is truth mediated by personality.

—Phyllis Brooks

The hidden curriculum . . . is the teacher's own integrity and lived conviction. The most memorable lesson is not what is written by the student on a sheet of yellow lined paper in the lesson pad; nor is it the clumsy sentence published (and "illustrated") in the standard and official text. It is the message which is written in a teacher's eyes throughout the course of his or her career.

—Jonathan Kozol

Every teacher teaches a curriculum. There's a state framework, state-approved texts, a district-approved curriculum, and a school's suggested approach to meeting that curriculum. But it still comes down to the teacher implementing the curriculum. The decisions a teacher must make about what students are to do and learn is fundamental to what it means to be a teacher. A teacher decides how much to emphasize phonics versus whole language reading, regardless of the public, political debate. A teacher decides whether to do art or math in the morning. A teacher decides whether to spend a week or three weeks on *Romeo and Juliet*. A teacher decides whether to test on Thursdays or Fridays. A teacher decides how to grade late papers. A teacher decides when to teach that $a^2 + b^2 = c$ and $E = mc^2$. A teacher makes these decisions based on what he or she understands to be important knowledge,

67

with full knowledge that he or she has to maintain discipline in the classroom and that he or she is subject to criticism by students, parents, administrators, and commissions. Our choices help define us as teachers.

There are four parts to this chapter. The first describes teaching as an
occupation that inevitably prizes literacy. The second describes teaching
as a complex and difficult job. The third section is my quintessential story
of what it means to teach the curriculum. It is the description of one of my
all-time greatest units, one that nearly got me fired. The fourth section is
about teaching the so-called hidden curriculum.

A SETTING THAT PRIZES WORDS

Frankly not all teachers are enamored with students. Like the stereotypical
librarian who prefers books to kids, some teachers prefer books. Having
said that, I want to say, too, that all teachers had enough affection for their
own experiences in school and particularly for the "language" of a given
subject(s) that they chose to become teachers. Sometimes we are a bit re-
sentful when our students do not share our affection for our subject matter.

There's something special, even remarkable, about the drawing good
enough to frame; about getting a base hit in the clutch; choosing the right
microscope lens and finding a previously unseen world; solving a particularly difficult equation; achieving that special insight into a book's character; realizing how history has a particular influence on your own family; being able to clearly share an opinion; or hearing a new piece of music
that you never forget. These are defining moments for us as students and
as teachers, and such moments do occur in the classroom.

At all grade levels I have had students tell me that a book they read for
me was the first that they had ever read. That is invariably both sad and
the high mark of teaching. The worry of teaching is in the worry of reaching too low and too high.

My first year of teaching, I purchased out of my own pocket a set of novels for the class that was based on the student's most popular TV shows of
the time. I still have ambiguous feelings about having done that. My students
could not read the texts that were on the curriculum, but it's also not feasible
for teachers to solve such problems out of their limited incomes. I bought the
set sight unseen, and was embarrassed by the poor quality of the writing. Yet

students who had not been reading read these books. And I was able to use that experience to teach other "English" concepts. With more experience I found better alternatives. That was, however, in my mind the most vivid example of my choosing material beneath what my students deserved.

On the other end of the spectrum, I still assign Ralph Tyler's *Basic Principles of Curriculum and Instruction* to my undergraduate class in education. And every year my students complain about it. "It's boring," they say. (At least it's short.) I've even considered giving up, but when I make the case for the book, my students invariably agree that they should read it because it's good for them, and that I shouldn't worry about their not liking it. I did stop assigning David Tyack's brilliant book *The One Best System,* because I became convinced the book could not be appreciated until students had actually served as teachers. With the Tyack book I had reached higher than I was able to successfully teach.

Every teacher knows the dilemma. Even a variety of relatively easy and relatively hard assignments must not be too easy or too hard. And our dilemma also reveals our implicit commitments to our field of knowledge. The novels that I bought for my class that were based on a TV series were not true to my feelings about the knowledge that I would most want to share; the example of the Tyack book was an overcommitment to my own biases and preferences without regard to students' stages of growth.

So, some teachers are easier than others, some more difficult. Some teachers read more than others, some talk more, but all of us decided to work in a field that prizes words. Did you know that a better prediction of a student's success than social class is print orientation in the home? I haven't seen any studies, but I'd predict that the children of teachers have better career success than would otherwise be predicted by parents' income.

Whether it is in finger painting, book reading, or public speaking, part of what is included in what it means to be a teacher is being comfortable in a setting that prizes words. One way or another all work together to help students become more fully literate in every sense of that term.

TEACHING IS DIFFFICULT

Despite the fact that this is a book written in appreciation of teachers, it is implicitly true that no student ever has the teachers they deserve. I've modified that line from the more common refrain, "No child has the parents they deserve." The truth of those lines does not represent a lack of regard for teachers. Rather it is a statement about how many adults it takes to help each of us realize, define, and explore our particular, unique personality.

After parents, and occasionally other adults in a family such as grandparents, students spend more time with teachers than with any other adults. While students spend much of their time defining themselves in comparison and contrast with their peers, they are at least looking over their shoulders at teachers for clues into the kind of adults they might become.

While this is natural, it is a huge, often unstated burden on teachers. Having about thirty students per class constantly using you as a measuring stick is a teaching opportunity, and an energy drain. A teacher's work is subject to constant and persistent criticism. (The way a teacher responds to that criticism is a great indication of how much that teacher can enjoy the job.) Seemingly every student has an opinion about whether you are too easy, too hard, too friendly, or too mean, smart or not smart, compared to every other teacher they have had.

While both the criticism and praise of teachers are often richly deserved, the point I would emphasize here is that very often, even most often, students are finding in us what they need. What they find may, indeed, be there, but perhaps it is not at all what we think we have offered. It is not uncommon for the students with whom we identify the most to need us hardly at all; it is not uncommon for students with whom we have less immediate rapport to latch onto us for reasons we scarcely understand. As I often say, I accept credit I don't deserve because I get blamed for things I didn't do. Some students need order, others freedom; some need a scolding, others praise; some need to be left alone, and others need inspiration. As teachers we do what we do, and with a little luck a student can pick and choose from each of us what he or she needs. Sometimes we are only negative examples. For example, many students realize they want to leave academia for business, where the financial rewards are more commensurate with their work.

But we are always an important part of the curriculum. We *humanize* the curriculum, with all the positives and negatives that it means to be human. "Curriculum" means "course," thus for teaching it means the course of study. The idea is that one develops strength while running the course.

Even the least effective teacher provides a course, a series of encounters, a field of experience. While we tend to remember both our most favorite and most despised teachers, all teachers provide us with access to some amount of education, both in the explicit curriculum of reading, writing, speaking, listening, and computing, and in the implicit curriculum, the socialization to certain standards of behavior that are either accepted or rejected. This role is supremely important—and it is very difficult.

As I stated earlier, my student teacher Trudy Crown observed, "You are never prepared for the amount of failure you experience as a teacher." She is absolutely right, and as I better realize over my decades in teaching (not that I like it any better) is that even our failures are an important part of the curriculum, part of the course, through which students define themselves.

When I complain about this, or about administrators, parents, or the students themselves, my friend and fellow teacher Mark McDonald asks me, "How do you feel about gravity?" (By the way, at one time in his career Mark would roller-skate off campus to his lunch.) Teaching is extremely difficult. The only advantage of that reality is that never truly mastering teaching keeps it interesting.

THE BEST OF TIMES, THE WORST OF TIMES

I believe I was a good curriculum teacher virtually from the start of my career. Teachers would brag in the English department office that they could get two things done in one class period. Through sheer energy I could consistently get four, and sometimes five, curriculum items done in one class period. I thought that was important. I read the *English Journal* from the National Council of Teachers of English voraciously, looking for ideas to use. I did, in fact, use a lot of their ideas. I looked through libraries, texts, and curricula from other schools and popular books. I was rather well informed and I often used others' ideas as a starting place for my own.

As a matter of fact, one of my best-organized units was one of my own design, influenced somewhat by Dan Fader's (1976) *Hooked on Books*. The students had read a few short stories they liked in an assigned text. When they tired of those stories, I brought my personal collection of short stories in from home and bought a large quantity of additional books containing short stories. I broke the collection (which included everything from ghost stories to sports stories, *Star Trek* to world classics) into thematic units, and let the students choose which groups they wanted to be in. Each small group had a set of core readings to do, as well as the option to read any story that might relate to their particular theme. Periodically I gave a discussion-type questionnaire that related to the theme.

Each group only had one copy of the questionnaire, so they had to figure out, as a group, how to complete the required task. The questions were designed to stimulate discussion. For example, the science fiction group had to make predictions on what the future would be like; the group on values had to react to hypothetical situations, such as: If a priest hears the confession of a murderer, should he turn him in? If your boat capsizes, do you save your child or spouse first? The assignments were brief, and designed to focus discussion on the relevant theme. The small groups worked together beautifully.

Besides the core list of stories that were required, each student was encouraged to read other stories that captured his or her interest. The students reported on each story they read by writing a short synopsis (as might be found in a television guide) and a short personal reaction. The synopsis was meant to teach such skills as summarizing, while the personal reaction placed emphasis on personal goals in reading. The students also kept a list of recommended stories, and although the lists per se did not work especially well, the students read an impressive number of stories because of other students' recommendations. Periodically I instructed students on the elements of the short story: plot, setting, point of view, characterization, theme.

About the only trouble I had with this unit came from an older member of the English Department. She complained because I had personally purchased many of the books the students used. She had a valid point. She argued that the school district was not going to provide funds if the teachers would. Does spending money from your own pocket delay necessary changes within the system? It is a good question. But at the time I was only anxious to prove what I could do, not change the system.

The only other real problem I had was keeping my books from being stolen. Students were enjoying reading, many for the first time, and most of them were reading lots. As the guy I voted against that year, Hubert Humphrey, might have said, "I was as pleased as punch."

Pasquel

During the short story unit I described above, which was going so well, the district supervisor of English teachers dropped in unannounced to visit my class. I do not remember exactly what we were doing that day, but I do remember it was going exceptionally well when the stern-looking man with the hawk nose, short-sleeved white shirt, polyester tie, and flannel pants entered my classroom. I was happy to have someone witness how smoothly a class could go at our notorious high school. Following class, I introduced myself to the silent visitor, who had not introduced himself. He told me his name was Pasquel and he was the district supervisor. I had no idea if that made him important or not, but in my enthusiasm for my new job and the efforts of my students, I naïvely shared some of the short stories my students had written. I was particularly excited by Louisa's short story, and I proudly showed it to him.

Making no comment on his observations of my class or the sensitivity with which Louisa's story was written, he asked me, "Why haven't you corrected her grammar?" Keep in mind this was the second month of school and one-third of my students were defined by the district as habitual failures. I indicated to him that it was still too early in the year to be correcting grammar on this kind of assignment; that I was more concerned the students felt they could freely express their ideas; that the assignment was more concerned with the total effect of a short story in terms of the concepts; and that even though I intended to do some work later in grammar, there was little support in the research that learning grammar per se had any relationship to writing literature.

I had thought about the reasons for not teaching grammar immediately at the beginning of a course and I listed these to him systematically. He responded that he expected me to teach grammar from the beginning. Not to be outdone, I indicated I had talked it over with Dr. Al Grommon, president of the National Council of Teachers of English (pulling rank) and with my department chairman (authorization) and that I had no intention of correcting grammar at this time on this kind of writing assignment. He did not like that attitude, of course, but he didn't offer a counterargument in support of his point of view. I assumed the issue had been dropped. As it turns out, Ron Baylor, the principal, later confided to me that Pasquel had tried to have me fired. Since Ron had never visited my class I believe

I was saved only by the reputation of competence that I had cultivated and that, fortunately, had been called to Ron's attention.

That a district person could drop in and upset my work without regard to my point of view was unsettling. At the time, I was apparently the first teacher ever to confront Pasquel and thus I gained a great deal of professional respect among my colleagues in the English Department. In retrospect, I understand I had violated powerful school norms. Teachers are supposed to publicly acquiesce to administrators knowing they have great freedom behind their closed classroom doors. An experienced, veteran administrator did not want to be "informed" of better ways to do things by an unproven rookie. But I am still appalled he tried to have me fired.

Teachers have a great deal of freedom behind classroom doors, but there are constraints—and these are not limited to district-approved texts or official courses of study.

TEACHING THE HIDDEN CURRICULUM

My friend Mark McDonald describes the rhetoric about education thus: "Skinner won; Dewey and Piaget lost." What he means is that the public pronouncements about education continue to emphasize (a la Skinner) behavior and learning (the kind of learning that can be measured by tests) instead of socialization and personal development (a la Dewey and Piaget). Of course, in reality, to sort out the academic teaching role from the developmental and socialization roles would be like separating heat and light: you can make light relatively cooler, and heat less bright, but you cannot separate them entirely.

Thus we try to teach knowledge *and* civilize our students. Meanwhile, especially with regard to socialization, students may have an entirely different agenda that is not entirely inappropriate.

Another friend, Raul Butterworth, who is an occasional anarchist as well as a teacher, said he was sending his own kids to Catholic school "so they would have something to rebel against." His own feeling was that Catholic schools more clearly defined the lines of authority than public schools. What he appreciated about that was that it was thus easier for the student to clarify his or her own, independent idea about obedience. As Raul is pointing out, our role as teacher includes socialization not only on our own terms; we also set standards to which students react in defining themselves.

Comedian George Carlin indicates that his career as a comedian was defined by his reaction to teachers more than his socialization to expected guidelines of behavior: "What better place," he reasoned, "to hone one's skills of making people laugh than in a setting where they are under such strict prohibitions not to do so" (Zehon & Kolter, 1993, p. 88).

While undoubtedly disrupting the classroom's academic lessons, Carlin, as well as the students who reacted to him, were defining their own relationships and reactions to authority. This is a necessary part of adolescent development.

And along the way George Carlin became educated. Undoubtedly each of his teachers made assignments that led to his becoming increasingly literate. Along the way his teachers helped him recognize the standards of conventional behavior. Teachers give most of the structure (cocurricular activities like sports and clubs make an important contribution as well) to a field of endeavor in which students are busily defining themselves. The "average" teacher is just as important in this regard as the inspirational teacher.

It took me nearly thirty years to learn an important lesson about inspirational teachers. I still feel entirely indebted to two of my high school teachers, John Daly and Alice Coleman. Consequently, as an academic advisor I have always encouraged my students to choose classes according to the teacher rather than simply by course title. But one semester I was too successful with my advice. In advising a group of college honors students, I was able to get almost all of them into four courses in the same semester with professors regarded as inspirational teachers.

Silly me. It was too much. These brilliant teachers competed for the attention of each student. It was virtually impossible for one of them to stand in the foreground with a background of the others. The net effect was that each tended to neutralize the effect of the others for this particular group of students. Why wasn't this apparent to me before? I have to hearken back to my theme that as a teacher we learn more from failure than success. But beyond that, part of the reason is that we spend all our time trying to improve education, and, that while that's important, we also need to spend time appreciating what already works.

The huge preponderance of teachers—even the ones we found boring or didn't like—structure and provide a field of endeavor that's more important than even family in giving us a place and experiences by which we can define our own public identities. Even the dropouts, whom we see as school failures, return to adult school and community colleges in record numbers. We have the most universal education in history and in the world. We do it a day at a time, setting a curriculum, setting standards for behavior. reacting to the diverse and divergent reactions of our students, and realizing that we are more a part of the process than ruled by some preordained student outcome. Why does it work as well as it does? As they say repeatedly in the film *Shakespeare in Love* about the success of art in the theater, "It's a mystery."

So we keep showing up as teachers and delivering our lines, and students grow in many, often unexpected, ways.

7

Every Teacher Has Memorable and Favorite Students

I'd rather learn from one bird to sing than teach ten thousand stars how not to dance.

—e. e. cummings

Where there is no sharing, there is no reality.

—Martin Buber

Teachers are most blessed by the number of special people they meet while carrying out their jobs. On rare occasions this special person will be an administrator or a parent; with luck it will be a teaching colleague; but certainly among the people who will bless a teacher's life there will inevitably be special students. While parents only have their own children, social workers have impossible case loads, and doctors see their patients so rarely, teachers have a great deal of interaction with others. Most adults are insulated in their jobs from the mutuality that comes with teaching—and working with thirty people on a daily basis in a contained space for a year. While some of the students a teacher works with will remain fairly anonymous, we meet some real characters. Some may drive us to occasional distraction, but even these certainly enrich our range of experiences of what it means to be human.

Rather than write pages about the saints who have come my way—the kind of students everyone appreciates as being exemplary human beings—I've decided to sketch some of the slightly offbeat characters who have made life more entertaining (not necessarily easier). Jenny Gray (1969, p. 94) says that it is the problem students who make us better teachers. The following were not exactly "problem" students, but they did strengthen me in important ways.

Every teacher has a set of memorable students. That's my emphasis here. This chapter is about the Davids, Eileens, Casses, Hanks, Harrys, Elvins, and Rauls. The chapter also includes my all-time favorite referrals that I have found in student cumulative folders. I end the chapter with a poem by a student, a poem so effective that I knew it by heart the first time I heard the student read it to our class.

MEMORABLE STUDENTS

Perhaps the very best part of teaching is the friends and/or characters the teacher first meets in the classroom. A handful of students become friends for life. With regard to the characters, I'm reminded of a supposedly Italian expression that goes something like, "Everyone loves the clown, unless he's your son." Over the span of a career, the cast of characters in a teacher's classes could fill the roles in a Fellini movie.

Every teacher has these memorable and favorite students. It is usually overlooked that presumably unpopular teachers are often popular with the presumably unpopular students. I once wrote a grant for an advising program that depended upon each teacher working with twelve to fifteen students. The students picked the teacher whom they'd like as an advisor. Despite my theory about every teacher having a following of special students, I was a bit worried that some teachers would not be selected. I shouldn't have worried. My prediction was correct. Even the "least popular" teacher was picked by thirteen students.

Thus I write with confidence that every teacher has a memorable gallery of these special students who make life richer. The following students are in my gallery of stars.

David

David Blacksmith was a comedian. Give him a difficult assignment and he would start telling jokes. Freddie Moran was a helper. Give him a difficult assignment and he would try to find something to do for someone else that would permit him to leave the class.

Most of my students had highly developed avoidance skills, but David amazed me most. He was supposed to be really "slow," and academically he was. But there was no one in the school who wouldn't stop and listen to his stories. When a teacher tried to make him do some work, he would tell the story about how he fell out of the football bleachers when he was a kid, a fall that he reported had caused him brain damage. His mother got some money from an insurance company on the premise he had been the victim of brain damage, but my research indicated he was no brighter academically before the fall than after.

I decided I wanted David to learn to read. Change that—David came to me and said he wanted to read. He wanted to be able to read a small book I had on an astronaut. Each day I would work with him on the book, and then he would work on his own. After five days, he could seemingly read the book aloud from cover to cover. But something puzzled me. The few words he missed, he was not even close on, and sometimes he read words that were in fact on the next page. I watched his eyes and discovered they were not moving from side to side. What David had done was memorize the whole reading. As the Sundance Kid said to Butch Cassidy about the tracker pursuing them, "I couldn't do that. Could you do that?"

David never learned to read very well. But he could read the notes I agreed to write and send home with him to his mother telling about the progress he had made in class. And he could read the stories he told me that I then typed up for him. The last time I saw David was at the end of the school year. He walked onto campus drinking a beer and inadvertently walked into the principal. He tried to tell the principal he had found the cold sweaty beer in the grass and was bringing it to him. David had some fine characteristics.

THE CUMULATIVE FOLDERS: EILEEN, CASS, AND HANK

Student cumulative folders are, of course, a great storehouse of valuable information. And they are permanent. I once found a paper airplane in a student's permanent file that contained a self-explanatory "Need I say more" referral to the main office on it. Ostensibly it was carried to the office

by the guilty party. Another great find was a referral for the "fourth of-
fense of eating sunflower seeds in class." The action taken was "D
NS3/5/69 DC-3/19/69" whatever action that might have been. Katie Kirkland got a referral and a letter home with this explanation: "The reason for
this is that she was burning incense in Girl's Chorus."

Eileen

A Student Behavior Referral on another of our students, Eileen Effram,
exemplifies one of the classic encounters between the regimen and the un-
regimented. Surprisingly, Eileen was able to write her own defense on the
referral form itself. Her defense was handwritten but this is how it read:

Student Name: <u>Effram, Eileen</u>
Grade: <u>10</u>
Subject: <u>P.E.</u>
Period: <u>2</u>
Date: _____

Senior High School Student Report—Student Behavior Referral
You have been sent to the Referral Desk for a particular discipline problem.
In order that the Vice Principal and/or Counselors know the extent of this
problem, fill out this sheet in detail. Be Specific! Be Honest! Be Fair!

Teacher: _____   Your Counselor: _____
Description of the problem:

The problem is I don't have any gym clothes. My mother doesn't have any
money to buy me some. She has barely enough to feed the kids. I am willing
to wear cut-offs and a white top but it will still count off on my grade so I'm
might as well not even get dressed. You people expect too much from people.
Why don't you start to love instead of making robots out of beautiful people.
You people are too materialistic. Why don't you all just let loose and be free.
I love you too.

Cass

An example from Cass's cumulative folder demonstrates the problems
that can exist between a teacher trying to do the best he can with a boring
basic math class (which the students did not want to take) and a student

who refused to go along with the program (as evidenced by the teacher's description of her "Adolph Hitler" type sneer). I don't doubt that within this context the teacher was acting appropriately in giving Cass a referral, but it is still funny.

The following teacher referral was taken directly from Cass's file:

In response to your disposition of referral of 2/23, please be advised of the following:

1. Takes every possible liberty to violate our rules and regulations governing classroom conduct. She is constantly leaving her seat to visit with her friends. These visitations are a real sore spot with me since they are most disruptive to a classroom overloaded with 80 marginal students whom we are determined to keep under control. When asked to take her seat (repeatedly) she renders a beautiful Adolph Hitler type sneer.

2. While at her seat continually engages in conversation with her neighbor and when asked to refrain from such activity, you get the same response as described above.

3. Is constantly involved in either the borrowing or lending of school materials in class. There is nothing basically wrong with these practices, except for the fact that it disturbs the class and always seems to "get things going."

4. Sure, Basic Math is boring work, but I think the importance of the subject should be brought out too. Also, she must be made aware of the reasons why she is in Basic Math to begin with, plus I tried to impress this upon all the kids at the beginning of the year, but apparently she gave us her usual deaf ear. My answer to this is that there is one way to beat this boredom and that is by working honestly and diligently through the course until you reach the pre-algebra and algebra section. Then things get interesting—new ideas new problems but she can't do the "interesting" stuff until you know the basics and she simply does not know the basics.

5. It is my estimation that she has one helluva chip on her shoulder. She has not displayed good citizenship in our class and at times she has not comported herself as a lady, not to mention the fact that she seldom dresses as one.

6. Any kid who makes the slightest effort in class work plus citizenship gets the benefit of the doubt in our class. She has not made the effort in the latter.

7. As far as "picking on her" is concerned, if one considers our demanding responsibility and respect as picking on a student, then I plead guilty.

8. The final blow in this whole episode came as a result of my refusal to let her sit in another location in the classroom. She sits where she is now because of her inability to work without entertaining her friends. I told her there were no seats available due to the size of the class and that I would not allow her to go back where all her friends are located.

Students like these are never boring.

Hank

Hank was a tall, dark, fairly handsome young man who loved to tell tall stories and lie about what he had or had not been doing with himself. He proudly told everyone he was part Indian, which may have been true. He also told us stories that seemed improbable, like the one about the time he "beat up two cops": "But I wasn't really trying to cause any trouble," he'd say. "In fact, when they were both out cold on the ground, I put their helmets and billy clubs right beside them, so they'd know I wasn't looking for any more trouble." Hank was tall and athletic, but I didn't believe him for a second.

I did believe he had trouble distinguishing letters, numbers, and words. Interested to discover why he might feel inclined to lie so much, but more anxious to see if he had a documented perceptual problem, I went to his cumulative school records. Hank had a most revealing school history.

I took the following notes from his cumulative file because I think they tell very clearly what happened to Hank. These notes were copied directly from his cumulative folder. Try to put the clues together yourself and solve what had happened to Hank, in school as well as at home. (I didn't make this up.) These were all comments recorded by school personnel and placed in Hank's permanent school cumulative file:

First Grade. Gets along well with others. Likes school. Very nervous. Large for age.

Second Grade. Mr. X says he can't catch a ball (large kick ball). May. Tires easily—poorly coordinated.

Fourth Grade. Good—interested parents. Extremely poor student.

Fifth Grade. January. Reverses words and numbers. Almost no sense of responsibility concerning school work, but is quickly helpful in other situations, often jumping up to help (open door, carry books, etc.) when he
is neither needed or wanted.

Sixth Grade. January. Parents don't know what to do. He has followed the
same pattern since he entered 1st grade. Dominance testing revealed that
Hank is right handed and left eyed. May. From parents: All privileges have
been taken away from him now until school lets out.

Seventh Grade. November. Hank's tests indicate that he has an above-average
intellectual potential, but is achieving far below his ability level, probably
due to a lag in perceptual maturation.

Ninth Grade. October. Notice to parents: Failure may result.

Eleventh Grade. October. Student's parent stated that he could do nothing
with Hank. Student will not attend school. Problem must be centered in
the home.

In fact I seldom referred to a student's file because I wanted to make up
my own mind about my students. I didn't want to be prejudiced by what
I might discover in my students' backgrounds. I would, however, resort to
the files at times, especially if I thought a student might have a physical
problem. Otherwise, I trusted my own assessment of students more than
the limited IQ tests, achievement scores, and teacher comments. After all,
many of my students had not tried on the tests, or in school, so I was skep-
tical of their files' accuracy.

In Hank's case I had looked at his file because I suspected he had a
perceptual problem that hampered his reading. The teacher comment in
second grade should have alerted the school system to the possibility of
such a problem: he couldn't catch a large ball. But regardless of any possible perceptual problem, we have on the testimony of his first-grade
teacher that Hank was a nice kid—he got along well with others. By second grade, however, we hear evidence of a possible defense mechanism
on Hank's part to protect himself from the judgment of his poor performance: "he tires easily," which is a good excuse for poor performance. By fourth grade, the record suggests Hank's parents had sided with
the school against Hank. Perhaps they were embarrassed by Hank's poor
performance. Invariably "good, interested parents" means the parents
hold their children, not the school faculty, responsible for their children's failures.

In fifth grade, Hank's file finally shows there was acknowledgement of his perceptual problem: he "reverses words and numbers." So it is not surprising that, after five years of extreme difficulty with the printed word, he had "almost no sense of responsibility for school work." But also notice Hank was apparently still trying to be the nice kid he was when he started first grade, and tried to avoid stress-causing classroom situations he knew he would fail by being overly helpful. How sad it must have been for the ten-year-old Hank to be neither "needed or wanted." By sixth grade he was causing trouble to avoid his academic problems. It should not have been surprising. The fifth-grade teacher had recognized Hank reversed words and numbers and in sixth grade, the district psychologist determined Hank was "right handed and left eyed." That factor seemed to be at the root of his perceptual problem with reading.

I didn't and don't have the medical background to know the "physical causes" of Hank's problems, but I was troubled to learn from Hank that his parents had insisted he be right-handed as a child, instead of following his natural disposition to be left-handed. Problems seldom have a single cause, but Hank's parents' desire for him to be as normal as possible—right-handed—may have significantly helped program Hank for failure. By sixth grade, the school knew officially that Hank had a serious perceptual problem, but by then, it was not only too late for Hank and school, it was too late for Hank and his parents. His "parents don't know what to do." In seventh grade, Hank had empirical proof he was no dummy. He had "above average intellectual potential." But educationally, the die had long been cast. Ironically, despite having taken the school's side from at least the fourth grade on, and having been "good, interested" parents, who also punished Hank for his school failures, the final school judgment before he came to us at Abraxas was that his problem "must be centered in the home."

How sad. Hank had tried everything. He had liked school when he started. But by second grade he tried to get out of work he couldn't handle. In fifth grade he tried to get out of work by being unnecessarily helpful. That was not appreciated so in sixth grade he tried hostility. By seventh grade he was passive (but without causing trouble to ensure promotion); when that no longer worked he started cutting school in ninth grade. He tried every strategy to avoid work he couldn't do. When we got him he had virtually no academic credits, although he was in his third year of high school. He clowned around when we pressured him to read or write. At first he lied compulsively, if he thought he might be in trouble with us. He had been extremely creative throughout his schooling in finding ways to avoid or excuse his academic deficiencies.

When we discovered verification of the perceptual problems, we tried some exercises we had read about that were being tried in Montessori schools. They offered a multiple-sense approach to words. We had Hank trace letters and words in a variety of ways. His reading skills improved rapidly and we tried to help him see what had unfortunately happened to him in school so he could accept himself better. But we could not solve his family problems and he joined the army midyear. We felt good about not contributing further to Hank's problems and having perhaps helped him some. I never found out if he returned from Vietnam safely, but I've never forgotten him.

PARENT CONFERENCES: THEIRS AND MINE

Virtually all of the stories in this book are told to communicate an impression of what it means to be a teacher. But this next story is told from a dual perspective, since I have had the great good fortune to have been a teacher and a dad. This story works a little better if you have seen the movie *Broadcast News* and remember the scene where Albert Brooks finally gets his chance to anchor a news program, to great comic effect.

As a teacher I always enjoyed making house calls, and I was never timid about parent conferences. For whatever sick and twisted reasons I enjoyed describing a child's behavior to a parent in a calm and rational, but specific, way. If you angrily told a parent their child had been cussing, invariably the parent would want to argue about what constituted cussing, and what did one expect with all that a child heard on television. But if you calmly and rationally told the parent that their child had called the school nurse a bastard and a son of a bitch, the parent would look shocked and grief stricken.

Another reason that these conferences generally went very well for me was that I was extremely successful in my commitment to finding something to like in all my students. I was also very adept at putting parents off guard. Right now I am particularly recalling asking the parents of two boys, two close friends, Harry and Elvin, to come in to see me. The parents obliged.

They had obviously been in to see teachers starting with kindergarten. They knew about their children, but were still prepared to defend them.

Even though Harry and Elvin were conspicuous challengers, they were also hilariously comic together. The character of their interaction is of the same stuff that makes Rowan and Martin, Lewis and Martin, the Smothers Brothers, and Abbott and Costello enjoyable to watch—but onstage, not necessarily in a classroom.

So, the two moms came in together. I was very confident even though I ordinarily would not see more than one set of parents at a time.

"Mrs. Clarke, Mrs. Aldrin, thanks for coming in. First, I want to tell you how much I like Harry and Elvin. Tell me the truth, they must make you laugh all the time?" I could tell that neither mom had ever had a school conversation that started on a positive note, which in no way means that I did not fully appreciate the exasperation felt by each teacher who had preceded me.

Lifelong friends, Mrs. Clarke and Mrs. Aldrin responded in one voice, which made it difficult to remember which woman supplied which words. "Oh, Mr. Gose, you have no idea, they pull something, and we are trying to scold them, and we are laughing so hard inside, it's not easy," they said.

"I know exactly what you mean. The class would be boring without them. They have so much energy. But sometimes I wish I could make them run a marathon before they came to class."

"Mr. Gose. You are so right. We feel the same way about them when they are at home."

The conversation continued and I brought in Harry and Elvin. We had a very nice chat, and determined that most all was right with the world. For the next while, the boys would sit separately in class, and try to be a little less rambunctious—which they were for a few days.

I had several years of such interactions with parents, and suddenly, after an excellent and stable teaching career, I was a parent on my way to my first parent-teacher conference. It was a beginning-of-the-year, individual parent-teacher conference. They had been scheduled for all of the school children over a week's period of time. As far as my wife and I knew, the start of the school year had gone fine for and with our daughter. The only snag had been before the school year had started. Our daughter had been assigned to one class, but there was talk of moving some of the kids to balance class sizes. We were happy with our assignment so we resisted a proposed change of teachers and we had been accommodated. Having been a teacher for so long I was concerned "our" teacher might have some residual feelings about our brief intervention.

The meeting was in our daughter's kindergarten classroom. I was not entirely comfortable in the pint-size chairs that we were offered. I was not completely comfortable period. It was a warm September day, but not so warm as to explain my discomfort. Now it was not simply my daughter, my child, we were to discuss, but Mrs. McPhee's student. I knew the multivariate range of things a teacher might feel obliged to tell a parent, yet I had no reason to feel dread. My child was great. She could read and compute before she started kindergarten. My nervousness was inexplicable, but it must have been related to not being the teacher. Now I was the parent. As we talked to Mrs. McPhee I began to sweat—profusely. I was sweating just like Albert Brooks in *Broadcast News,* except instead of having someone from off-camera wipe my face during the breaks, my wife would reach over anytime Mrs. McPhee looked away and wipe my brow. It was entirely embarrassing. My shirt was soaked, the knees of my slacks were wet, my hair became matted, and the perspiration ran profusely, streaming down my face. More than twenty years later I still cannot fully account for my physiological reaction. But there's something in it about what it means to be a teacher and a parent.

Raul Munoz

Have you seen *Bambi Meets Godzilla?* It's a classic animated short subject film. To the sounds of lovely music, Bambi is feeding in an idyllic setting. Suddenly a giant foot descends from the top of the screen and crushes the little doe. It represents an archetypal conflict. Even before I had seen this great animated short, one of my students, Raul Munoz, waxed eloquently on the same theme.

Flitter Flutter

Flitter, flutter in the mist,
Comes the Butterfly, I tried to pet it, but instead,
He hit me in the eye.
And so I grabbed the damn thing,
and threw him on the dirt.

> I stepped on him with all my might,
> And watched his guts go squirt.
> *by Raul Munoz*

'Tis one of the few poems I have ever unintentionally memorized. It just sounds right. Every teacher has countless such memories of special students.

8

Certain Administrators

Every teacher runs up against frustrating authority figures. Every teacher can cite countless examples of inexplicable behavior by persons who were presumably thought capable of administrating a school. Their slights are always more difficult and problematic than those from students, because, at least ostensibly, administrators are hired to help teachers, not drive us crazy. Certainly it's not true of all administrators, but to teachers most all do seem capable of folly.

I have often wondered why administrators have such a powerful effect on morale. After all, one of the greatest aspects of teaching is the freedom we have behind the classroom doors, where most of our work is basically positive and constructive. But it seems it is stories about administrators that we need most to get off our chests.

THREE STORIES

I tell three stories here. The first is about a vice principal, who was also the varsity baseball coach; the second is about a vice principal simply being a vice principal; and the third is about a principal. Each story is about my rebellious relationship, as a teacher, with the given administrator. Most teachers are less rebellious, but they certainly will understand the frustration, and are likely, at least privately, to smile about my willingness to do battle with these administrators.

Peter

My most famous altercation with a vice principal was audacious for a first-year teacher. I was coaching the freshman baseball team, a very low-status position. For two hundred dollars, I spent from February 1 to June's school end working with about fifteen fifteen-year-old baseball players. It was really quite a lot of work, so I did not expect harassment from the varsity baseball coach, who was also the vice principal. I didn't know about rookies paying hardship dues. I assumed he would appreciate having me around, and my putting up with poor scheduling, threadbare uniforms, and miserable equipment. As if these conditions were not enough to remind me of what a low-status position I had, the varsity coach reminded me each day by stealing the few baseballs I had from my ball bag.

At first I could not believe that it was he who was responsible. A varsity baseball coach, who also served as the "boys'" vice principal, stealing baseballs out of my ball bag? My first reaction to the missing baseballs was to suspect that someone was breaking into the lockers. I went to this varsity coach, Peter Hamm (the kids called him Arnold the Pig), and expressed my concern over the missing balls. I told him how distasteful I found it to have to spend the first fifteen minutes of practice trying to scrounge up baseballs. He grinned wryly. Eventually I began to figure out what was going on. The only appropriate word to describe my locker-room reaction was "pissed."

Once I had it figured out, I really looked forward to the next day's practice. Admittedly, I hoped the baseballs would once again be missing from my ball bag; I hoped they would be being used on the varsity diamond because I had a plan. I had asked Peter several times to prevent the baseballs from being "liberated." He had the only key to the equipment locker and the wry smile. Whether he was stealing the baseballs or permitting them to be stolen, it was all the same to me. I approached the situation with righteous indignation. And my team was in on the plan. We had marked our baseballs so that there was no question as to whom they belonged.

Sure enough, the next day the baseballs were gone from my ball bag. My first baseman checked the varsity diamond and sure enough, the marked baseballs were there. Unlike other days when I had to go grovel for my fair share, I broke out the varsity's new game balls. The varsity team only got two new balls for each league game and when they were finished, we used them for our games. But this time my players were warming up for an ordinary practice by throwing around the precious brand-new baseballs. The whiteness of the balls lit up the whole field between the varsity and freshman diamonds. Delightedly I watched the varsity coach send a runner down to me. His runner told me that Coach Hamm said they were his game balls and asked for them. I requested the player to convey my humble apology to the coach, but they were the only baseballs I had. Sorry.

I did not lose any baseballs after that. I felt great. Sometimes I think, perhaps gleefully, maybe I *am* a troublemaker.

Rudy

Near the end of one first semester, I received a note that John Jones or somebody with such a name was transferred to my class. John Jones never showed. A couple of weeks later, I was asked to give a semester transfer grade to John Jones. I tried to tell the vice principal, Rudy Sapparro, that I could not give a semester grade to a student I had never seen. Rudy said, "Flunk him." That did not set real well with me so I tried to reason with him. I tried to explain I could not in good conscience do that. But I did not seem to be getting across, because no matter what I said, Rudy responded, "Flunk him." He gave no other response to my ideas—he just repeated "flunk him."

Upset that a vice principal would talk to me that way, I took my complaint to our principal. You may remember the principal I mentioned who gave the opening remarks to new teachers? This was the man who gave us all a history of his career. He had reached a crisis where his wife had told him he would have to give up coaching baseball or give up her. Ron said he had thought about it for a while and sometime later decided to give up baseball. He handled this problem judiciously as well. Ron told me he did not like Rudy either—the perfect answer.

Every teacher has such experiences of administrators, and we wish that they didn't annoy us so much.

Mr. Bonaview

Before I go further in my indictment of certain administrators—and I'm not trying to be particularly fair here anyway—I will confess that from time to time I've been an administrator. On occasion I've done some stupid things myself, some of which were not entirely without some cause.

A particular example that I still feel ambivalent about is the use of the school public address (PA) system. Like all teachers I was always annoyed by the disruption. So as an administrator, I was committed to minimizing disruptions of classrooms by the use of this system. Well, I thought I was committed.

Bureaucrats who pass legislation about what school *must* do are often entirely unaware of the limits of what schools *can* do. At this time there was a law passed requiring schools to test every student. It does not really matter for this story what we were testing, just that we were required by law to test each and every student. The major problem with this law is that the students were not required by law to take this test. And is there anyone who knows anything about teenagers who doesn't know that some percentage of teenagers will resist doing anything that is required, much less anything they do not want to do?

Those who skipped the tests and makeup tests were still required to take the exam or the whole district would be in trouble. There was a threat our funding would be cut, and even though I didn't believe that, all the other administrators did. This group of students also proved another of my "laws," that is, the last 10 percent of a project takes up about 90 percent of the time. And we had a deadline.

I devised a solution that "worked." Much to the chagrin of the teachers who had begun to think they could trust me, I interrupted the entire school each period by announcing the names of all the students who needed to come to the front office. By Friday we had seen them all. Was it worth it? In terms of Maslow's "needs hierarchy," yes. Our funding was at stake. In terms of education? No way.

My supposition, then, is that there must be times when administrators make frustrating decisions, but with mitigating circumstances. But having tried to be at least that fair, I'll say that most teachers at some, if not most, times in their careers have had to adjust their understanding of what it means to be a teacher to the reality that administrators have a huge impact on morale, and that impact is often very frustrating.

Administrators are responsible for a variety of situations: The new classroom with the big windows and blinding sun, for example, for which shades are never obtained; the insistence that all classroom doors remain shut regardless of whether that classroom's air conditioner works or whether the room has a heater that comes on only in the summer; an insufficient number of texts for the number of students assigned to a class; a new program *required* without teacher input, consent, or sufficient preparation; poor choices in hiring; lack of support against bullying parents; more frowns than smiles; impossible deadlines; poor scheduling; embarrassing public presentations; and petty expectations.

These are just some of the chronic problems teachers must cope with in regard to some administrators. As a teacher I was only surprised the first time one of my "confidential" memos was widely distributed; the first time I was assigned more than my share of problem students because I was perceived as being successful; the first time I was told to close the door to my unbearably hot classroom; the first time I was asked to turn something long in by that Friday; the first time I was blamed for something I hadn't done.

My last story about frustrating administrators is also about my own difficulty in coping. It's an example that ends up showing my own immaturity, and my own passive-aggressive behavior. Yet with added maturity, I suspect I'd still do the same thing; I knew then that my behavior was childish. But I do think the story contains an important underlying message about what it comes to mean to be a teacher.

In defense of my behavior, I want to say, first, that thirty or so children in a classroom exert more of an influence on the teacher than the teacher is likely to exert on them. As teachers we have had modeled for us a wide range of immature strategies for reacting to authority, and it is more surprising how seldom we resort to such behavior than how often we do. Second, despite how much we feel in control of our own classrooms behind closed doors, or maybe especially *because* we feel so in charge of our classrooms, teachers particularly resent the intrusions into that identity by administrators, who all too often treat us as children.

So, I want to end this chapter by telling about Principal Bonaview. The only truly unmixed expression of support that I can say for him is that I needed that job and he did not overrule the personnel director who determined to hire me. Mr. Bonaview struck everyone at first by his seemingly milquetoast personality, yet rumor had had it that at a much earlier age he had been a Gold Gloves boxer. Word also had it that his wife put his clothes out each morning so that he would know what to wear.

At this school, students were allowed to play music at the nutrition break. Those of us on supervision duty were alarmed one day to see Mr.

Bonaview enter the quad with a visitor at the exact moment the student disc jockey put on the Woodstock album (they still had albums then) with the cut where Country Joe and the Fish spell out the "F word." We didn't need to be alarmed—the song passed right over his head.

Mostly Mr. Bonaview was the source of petty annoyances. There was nothing that we resented more than his single-minded commitment to greeting us individually and personally each morning before school started, at the nutrition break, at lunch, and at the end of the school day. Perhaps at first all this attention from the principal seemed nice, but the daily routine felt intrusive, even threatening.

The prospect of threat from Mr. Bonaview was proven when he fired our art teacher. He could do this fairly easily because the art teacher was on probationary status. Rob was a young and charismatic art teacher who had immediate success with some of our most troublesome students. Perhaps Mr. Bonaview resented Rob's success. In any instance, Mr. Bonaview complained loudly, publicly, and to everyone but Rob about the way Rob dressed and the messiness of his classroom. The staff figured it was okay for him to wear the same clothes for a week since he was a hands-on teacher, at the bottom of the pay scale, who was getting paint and clay all over himself.

He also had a fatal flaw: he liked to clean up his classroom in the morning before class started rather than at the end of the day when he was tired. Unfortunately for Rob, Mr. Bonaview liked to visit his classroom in the afternoon after Rob had left. Mr. Bonaview took such exception to the condition of the art classroom that he fired Rob in the middle of the semester.

Perhaps to his surprise Mr. Bonaview was told that the staff was upset by this peremptory decision. I was more than a little alarmed when he called me in to his office, presumably for damage control. I was not sure, and remain unsure to this day, whether he was calling me in to his office as a sign of respect or to warn me that I was next in line. I dressed well and kept a tidy room, but I was also popular with students. Maybe that, too, was a fatal flaw.

It was a short speech Mr. Bonaview gave me. I intended as I heard it to remember it exactly so that I could report it to the staff members. But his one-sentence thesis mixed several metaphors and alas my memory failed to remember the order in which they were used. He said:

"We are not bound to the ties of the shackles of tradition." Or maybe "We are not tied to the binds of the shackles of tradition." Or was it "We are not shackled to the ties of the binds of tradition"? Or "We are not shackled to the binds of the ties of tradition," No—"We are not bound to the shackles of the ties of tradition." Or "We are not tied to the shackles of the binds of tradition."

Whichever way he said it, the message was very clear: we were, in fact, tied, bound, and shackled to the ties, binds, and shackles of the ties, binds, and shackles of tradition. And my conclusion was that I'd better look for a new job for the next year.

Meantime, some response was necessary, a response that would make a statement, but not cause me to lose me my job: I decided on civil disobedience. Well, maybe not so much civil disobedience, since I didn't feel civil and I hated the trouble disobedience can cause. But it was something of a crusade.

None of my colleagues could ever remember a time that they had not been tracked down and greeted several times a day by Mr. Bonaview. He was compulsive about it, which was part of the reason no one ever felt truly greeted. I determined to go an entire day without his having seen me, which was no small test since my classroom was in the same building as his office. But the building did, at least, have two entries/exits.

Bonaview typically started the morning at the faculty parking lot, observing the coming and the going of his staff. To his credit Mr. Bonaview would not interrupt a class while it was in progress, so I had four windows of opportunity to miss him all together: before and after school, at nutrition break, and at lunch time.

Before school was the easiest. I parked at the front of the school, came in the front door, went immediately to my classroom, and shut the door. I heard him in the hallway just before class started, but the bell rang before he got to my room. I was 25 percent there. The nutrition break was more of a gamble. Instead of following my usual pattern of going to the quad, I simply stayed in my classroom. He never thought to look for me there. Already my great friend and colleague Bart Walton was telling the other teachers the saga, the tale, that I was half way there.

Bart assures me that I was the topic of the lunchtime conversation among my colleagues. Would I prevail, would I be successful? I certainly had the prayers, best wishes, and complicity of my colleagues. At lunch I waited until a knock on my door by Bart assured me that Mr. Bonaview had gone to the quad. I went out the front door to my car and went off campus to lunch. The trick was getting back to my classroom after lunch. Five minutes before class was to start Bart agreed to occupy Mr. Bonaview with an ostensible discipline problem. I came back to my classroom by the front door. I was safe!

I only had fifth and sixth period to go. I held fifth period beyond the bell until members of sixth period began arriving. I was safe again, and Mr. Bonaview did remain consistent in refusing to interrupt class. It was the stuff of legends. I came, I saw, I conquered. All that remained was the rush to the car after the final bell.

I was keyed up; it was one of the rare times in my career that I was distracted while teaching. The final bell rang, the students fled, and I was left to my destiny as I stared at my closed classroom door. I stood there for moments, staring at the door and giving great thought to climbing out my window. We were on the first floor, and climbing out would guarantee my success and my fame. Mr. Bonaview ordinarily supervised the loading of the school buses. But did I dare risk my full day's success? No other teacher had made it even this long, but the effort, in memory of Rob, our dearly departed art teacher, was to finish the entire day without having been encountered by the man.

Eventually I determined that I would have to test fate, that as much as I wanted to climb out the window, it would be a cowardly act. I flung open the door.

"Good afternoon, Mr. Gose."

I am certain that his two feet were exactly even with the door frame, and that if I had slammed the door hard enough, and if it had any give, it would have broken his nose. He was standing that close to being within the actual door frame.

But what could I do? Or say? I had lost. At least I could lose gracefully.

"Good afternoon, Mr. Bonaview."

Because teachers, whether by nature or by adaptation, must be long suffering. And we are bound to the ties of the shackles of tradition, each and every one of us. God bless us all.

9

Dilemmas

For every person wishing to teach there are thirty not wanting to be taught.

—W. C. Sellar

I'll call them "conundrums." Some aspects of teaching are predictable: you won't have the right number of textbooks, there will be gum under every desktop, some student's only goal will be to get your goat. But just as soon as a teacher has developed a routine to handle most of the issues that are likely to occur for their subject and grade level, a problem will arise that has no obvious solution. These are the conundrums that try teachers' souls. The challenge of finding a solution for a previously unencountered dilemma helps define a teacher's development.

PERPLEXING STORIES

Here are some stories of situations that perplexed me, along with my "solutions." I offer them all with the realization that different teachers would have reacted differently, but that through our decisions we develop our individual identities as teachers.

Baseball

Two of my toughest incidents as a teacher occurred while I was coaching. They both were with students, not other coaches. I think most coaches would have handled the incidents differently than I handled them.

I could have won the league championship in baseball with the freshman team I was coaching. Ron Putin, who later played football with the New York Jets, was our catcher and team leader. Ron had enormous potential as a baseball player as well. He was too good to play freshman baseball so I sent him up to junior varsity just after the season began. It wasn't really a hard decision to send him up. As badly as I wanted to win the championship, I would not have considered holding any player back. Besides, we still had excellent pitching and a good backup catcher. And except for two incidents, we would have won the championship.

The first involved white shoes. At that time, everyone in baseball wore black shoes, everyone except the Oakland A's, an American league team about to win three consecutive World Series. They wore white shoes and were famous for their nonconformity. My infield wanted to dye their shoes white and came to me asking if they could. I knew the junior varsity and varsity coaches would not approve, but I felt it was a decision for my team, not the other coaches. Besides, I liked the A's and their long hair, white shoes, and winning ways. My players decided our team didn't want all white shoes, but anyone who wanted to dye their own shoes white could. So my starting infield decided they would.

Friday at 3:24, my starting infield was nowhere to be found for our 3:30 game. They arrived at 3:25, white shoes in hand. They were much too late for the pregame warm up. They had had to go home (without telling me) to pick up their newly dyed shoes, which had not dried by school time that morning. Their lateness was an obvious breakdown in team discipline. The team was still in position to win the league championship. If I went ahead and started my infield, I felt sure we'd win the game at hand, even if they did only have five minutes to warm up. But I submitted my starting lineup without their names. I benched them and I didn't tell them for how long. I kept them out four innings of the seven-inning game because I reasoned the bench deserved to play longer than the starters. After four innings we were losing 5-0. We lost the game 5-4. We fell into a tie for first place. We all ran wind sprints after the game, including me, because

I reasoned we had had a total team breakdown. And we still had full opportunity to win the championship despite that one game.

The second incident revolved around a league rule. It was a good rule that most kids didn't appreciate: you couldn't play in two baseball leagues at the same time. I recently read about an orthopedic surgeon who x-rayed the arms of ninety kids who had pitched Little League baseball. Eighty-four evidenced arm damage. The league rule was designed to protect our players. Even if one disagreed with the rule, it was still the rule that anyone playing in two leagues was to be dropped from the high school team. Despite the fact that our league rule was well known, the local Pony League insisted on beginning their season while our season had two weeks to run. I warned my players, as I had at the beginning of the season, that they should not play in the other league until our season was over, that we only had four games to go and still had a good chance of winning our championship.

My players argued (accurately, by the way) that the other teams in the league ignored the rule and had never been punished (theoretically, but only theoretically, a team was supposed to forfeit any game in which they had used an ineligible player). I explained it was meant to be a good rule to protect their arms and even if they disagreed, it was a rule, and as a teacher, one I especially had to respect. Nonetheless, my best pitcher, my starting shortstop, my starting centerfielder, and my starting first baseman played in another league. They were such excellent players I am confident that there was a lot of pressure on them to play in this other league.

Naturally I found out. I asked them if they were playing in another league and they admitted it. I told them I had no hard feelings, just disappointment, and they accepted, if didn't understand, when I dropped them from our team with three games to go. It especially hurt to drop the All League pitcher, who would have pitched two more games. We lost our last three games and finished in a tie for second place, two games behind the champion. We could have won the championship. I had hoped to win it anyway, but without two of our best players we came up short. Even after the season we might have won the championship.

The championship team had used players who had also been playing in the Pony League. My pitcher and first baseman and a couple of other players on my team came and told me. They wanted me to protest. With the three forfeits they would have had, we would win the championship. I told them I had done what I felt necessary because it was right and that I didn't want to win that way. When I asked them if they did and were willing to testify, they agreed with me that it was no way to win a championship.

I wanted that championship very badly. A part of me wanted to play the late, white-shoed players and my best players at the end of the year. I wouldn't have even minded someone else exposing the championship team and giving us the championship trophy. But Lombardi was wrong— winning's not the only thing.

Katie

One spring day, Bart and I realized we had had it with Katie Kirkland. As codirectors of the program she was enrolled in, we had resisted and endured her nasty temperament (read "bitchiness") as long as we could. She needed only fifteen units and to pass the math proficiency test to graduate early. We doubted we could make it to June without our doing her grave bodily harm, so we conspired.

"Katie. We hadn't realized how close to graduation you are. You only need 15 units," I said.

"So?" she replied.

"Hey, it's up to you. We just wanted you to know we wouldn't hold you back since you're ahead of the others," I told her.

"Yeah, I wouldn't want to advertise this, but if you finished early, you'd have a head start looking for a summer job. I don't want you yelling at me in June when you realize you could have taken a job earlier," Bart added.

Katie squinted at us.

"What if I want to stay?" she asked.

"Hey, we need your attendance, we'd just as soon you stayed," we lied.

"Well, I'm tired of this scene. When can I go?"

We told her what she'd have to finish in order to graduate. Ten days later she was done, with the exception of the math proficiency test. It was a forty-question test, and Bart administered it. She took it alone in the back room. Frankly, Bart and I hoped she'd cheat if necessary. She brought the test back to us with a wide gleaming smile on her face. She waited expectantly. His face became flushed. She'd answered four of the forty questions correctly. He didn't tell her the total, but he did tell her she'd failed. She handled the conflict in her conventional manner evidencing no behavioral progress for all our efforts.

"That's a bunch of shit," she said as steam escaped from her ears.

"Katie," Bart tried to calm her.

"This school's full of crap."

"Katie."

"I shouldn't have to take such a dumb test."

"Katie."

"God, I hate school."

"Katie."

"I'm quitting. I just can't take this shit anymore."

"Katie. You can take the test again tomorrow," Bart said.

"Tomorrow's Friday. I don't come on Fridays."

"Well, you can do it next week."

"I'll be here tomorrow."

Bart gave her some practice sheets and Katie took them reluctantly. She returned the following morning optimistically, smiling.

"I just had a bad day yesterday. I know I can do that crap." Bart gave her the test and sent her to the back room to complete it. She returned a while later with her customary "optimism."

"How'd you do?" I asked tentatively.

"Well, I hope I passed," she answered excitedly. You next need to know I was closer to wringing her neck than Bart, but it was Bart who graded her paper. As he graded the paper, he winced and without moving his head, looked at me out of the corner of his eye. His look told all. Then he made his own existential decision. I never looked at her test to know anything different than what he announced.

"Katie, you know you needed thirty correct answers to pass don't you?"

"Yes," Katie answered tentatively, her voice strained.

"You got thirty right."

Katie shrieked.

"Can you believe it? Can you believe it?" she asked me and the other few students who were there. "What luck. What luck! I'm done!"

"Congratulations," I offered.

"I'm done! I'm done."

"What now?" I asked.

"Oh, I'll get a job. My mom'll be so happy."

This is not, however, the end of the story. The following Monday morning I went by Winchell's Donut House to buy our customary Monday donuts. Much to my surprise and anguish, Katie was behind the counter. It was too late to avoid her and go elsewhere. I smiled and greeted her pleasantly.

"Katie. You've already gotten a job."

"Yeah," she said flatly.

"Did you have it lined up before?"

"Nope. I got it Saturday."

"That's great. Could I have two glazed and two French crullers?"

She waited on me pleasantly enough. I gave her a five-dollar bill. As she gave me my change, I slowly realized she'd shortchanged me. I didn't care. There was justice in the world. Bart and I deserved to suffer for our inability to teach her to count. We'd gotten our just rewards. I couldn't wait to get to school to tell Bart the story. I laughed at us all the way to school, waiting to tell Bart what had happened.

Distant postscript: During one of the clashes with Katie, when I would not let her shoot arrows in the direction of houses, I wrote her a long letter denying her accusation that a personality clash was the only clash we were having. To be fully responsible to her, I wrote, I felt I had to get her to look at her attitude. Three years later, after I had left the district, Katie arrived at the school looking for me. She had kept the letter those three years, she said, she had paid attention to its contents, and she did appreciate what I had had to tell her. I was grateful and humbled to receive that message.

Carrie

I do not, at least theoretically, believe in what is often referred to as "situational ethics." I believe there generally is a right and a wrong and that the ends don't justify the means. So I can't justify my actions in the story I am about to tell, even if my church's minister, youth minister, and some college-aged parishioners did conspire with me. I will say we had a lofty goal, though: we hoped to ensure that one of my graduated seniors, who had overcome financial challenges to earn admission to a prestigious East Coast college, would be able to fly, space available, to her destination.

Of course what we all should have done was simply chip in and pay the difference between a standby fare and a normal fare. However, as I've described elsewhere, teachers do not have surplus income, nor do ministers or college students. And there was joy in such wickedness as we were to commit. I realized that if each of us made a reservation for the air flight the student was trying to get on—or several reservations, maybe even many reservations for that particular flight—she would undoubtedly be able to get on it with a standby ticket, space available. My church friends conspired with me. We made voluminous reservations. (Undoubtedly it was behavior such as this that caused airlines soon thereafter to change their rules about reservations.) To our credit we did not let her know what we were doing. She was to benefit from our sin without complicity.

We made our reservations, left our individual names, left our individual phone numbers, and gosh, as it turned out, none of us ended up being able to make that particular flight. My former student, who had never even flown before, made the first flight for which she tried without having to wait hours, or even days, for a flight that would start her new academic venture.

This is the same sort of callous conscience that so many of us develop. It is most often seen in our willingness to violate copyright restrictions. We will ensure that we do whatever we can for our students, at least if the probability of our getting into a lot of trouble is remote.

Quick Freddie

Two of our graduates technically should not have graduated. Quick Freddie was known as Quick Freddie because of the way he drove his yellow Camaro Super Sport and for the way he "operated" with the school's young women. Despite, or perhaps because of his reputation, he was universally liked by students, teachers, and even administrators. He was blond, handsome, and short. He had a disarming grin that made you want to believe him even when, during one of his many cruises through the school parking lot, he had laid rubber for the umpteenth time and apologized to you for putting you on the spot and having to yell at him for his immature behavior.

His counterpart was something of an opposite. Tall, dark, unkempt, sullen, maybe even morose, this student carried a hunting rifle in the rear window of his large, metallic blue, raised, four-wheel-drive truck. (I politely, nicely, beseechingly asked him not to bring the rifle to school anymore and he generally didn't.)

Despite their differences in style these two students had much in common. For one thing, the two students both failed the English proficiency exam the first year it was given in the district. I can't imagine either of these two students ever having passed the exam. Neither was academically inclined, and neither had what the district termed "minimum essential skills for adult survival." What was unique, however, about these two seniors was that they each were making more money annually than any of their teachers. (And no, they weren't selling drugs.) They both farmed. They leased land and grew produce for market, and paid an accountant and secretary as necessary to perform their basic skills. Both cleared over $50,000 a year while still attending school full-time. Should they have graduated? Were they without minimum essentials? Fortunately, the California state requirement for testing of basic skills for graduation was still one year away. The superintendent was able to waive the district's self-imposed requirement and both students graduated with their class.

However, I always wondered what would have happened if they had been in school one year later and had been required by law to pass the proficiency exam to graduate. Both students' parents were highly influential in the community. Who could argue with the students' proficiency at "survival" skills? They were already "successful." I suspect the school district would have found some other way of waiving the requirement. Whether these two students should or should not have graduated, I resist any set hurdle, test, grade point average, years of experience, that everyone absolutely must meet without exception.

GRADES

In this chapter on dilemmas, my emphasis is that one of the important ways that a teacher defines her- or himself is by the response to decisions that must be made and that cannot be anticipated. Of all the chapters of this book, this one certainly includes stories of individual decisions. Other teachers may not have done the same thing in the given situation, but teachers will understand the deliberation that comes with making hard choices.

I have almost never had student teachers consider the circumstances that I will now describe and come to the same decision. Nonetheless, in retrospect I am even proud of the decisions that I did make in these circumstances. I do consider them defining moments in my career. Both examples came from my first year in teaching.

These are examples about grading students. I've certainly had more sleepless nights about grades than about any other dilemma. Eligibility for sports, passing to the next grade, graduation, college scholarships, and a beating at home are only some of the more obvious consequences of grades. The grades a student earns are a lot more subjective than anyone likes to admit, even if it is the teacher's subjective decision to "curve" grades instead of relying on a strict point system. Two memorable students caused me to wrestle with my own conscience regarding grades. (I talked a little about both of these students in chapter 4.).

Will, a tenth-grader in my sophomore English class, had nothing to distinguish himself the first month of school. Then he was in a fairly serious car accident and I went to visit him a couple of times in the hospital. I took him homework once he was able to do it. That small gesture on my part seems to be related to the development that once he returned to school he became a ball of fire in my class. By the end of the semester he had earned enough points for a B+.

Ennis learned to love reading in my English class. He read dozens and dozens of books—good books but books written particularly for teenage readers. Ennis was also an extremely nice kid. He was very responsible; he did all his homework; he helped whenever and wherever he could. I even made him "manager" of my frosh-soph baseball team. But academically Ennis was not very accomplished. He had never had a grade higher than a C. Yet he was the best-loved student in my class. And he had only enough points for another C.

What grade did I give Will? What grade did I give Ennis? The first grade that I wrote down on Will's report card was, indeed, a B+. But having written it down, I found that I couldn't live with that grade. Eventually I found my rationalization. Will had the highest B+, so I curved the grades and he had an A−, which is what I changed the grade to.

On Ennis's grade card I wrote the "C." And I couldn't live with that either. He had learned to love to read. He wasn't college bound, so the grade I gave him would give him no false information about his chances to go to college. This was probably the class that he would have enjoyed most in his entire school life. I changed the grade to an A.

These are perhaps the only two times I ever made such decisions about grades. But I've had no regrets—quite the opposite. A year later I would read in a Jim Herndon book (1971, p. 88) his assertion, "it is the teacher who puts the grade down on the report card." A teacher comes up with a grading policy to be as fair as possible and to protect against bias. But at the young ages of twenty-one and twenty-two, I came to a realization of how a teacher spends an entire life figuring out issues of right and wrong. In these two instances I wrote down the A– and A, and I remain defiantly glad that I did.

These are the moments that define what it means to be a teacher, and although we teachers are not likely to come to the same conclusions, we do realize the importance of this struggle.

Honor and Betrayal

No man is a prophet in his own country.

—The Gospel of Matthew

Teachers constantly face both honor and betrayal—often on the same day. Probably no other role other than parenting is as fraught with such ambiguity. This will be the book's shortest chapter. As I've thought about this issue I've realized that while this is a defining reality of being a teacher, it's the hardest to tell stories about. The realizations of both honor and betrayal are so personal that the individual stories are not as representative as the feelings themselves. Suffice it to say that stories of honor and stories of betrayal are suggestive of the constant reality of how teachers face both highs and lows on a regular basis.

HONOR

Denise's poem, which follows, is representative of the messages that teachers sometimes receive. These messages are usually an honor that we never feel we have truly earned. The value of such occasional tributes cannot be underestimated for their encouragement and value.

To: Mr. Gose
To a great person,

I shall not forget.
If I never met you,
I'd be so upset.
I felt no one cared,
If I wrote, or I died
But you made me feel
Once again so alive.
I knew someone cared
For something I did.
I felt so proud
I began to feel big.
So thank you a million
Stay cool as you are
As a friend, as a teacher
You're going to go far.
Love always, Denise Navarra

BETRAYAL: MARIJUANA AT THE CLASS CAMPING TRIP

I took one of my favorite classes on a camping trip and had a bad experience that distressed me greatly. It showed me the disparity between the teacher role and the student role, regardless of how well I seemed to communicate as a teacher with students. I always insisted on taking only students I knew on camping trips, but one trip, my very favorite students begged me to let their friend Moe come, too. When a couple of other students dropped out of the trip, I relented. I always made all my students swear they would not take any alcohol or drugs on our trips, and this was the only trip where I ever had a problem.

The night before we were to return home, a friend of mine, Harry, who had come on the trip to drive and help chaperone, told me he had seen Moe smoking marijuana down by the creek. I couldn't believe it. I asked Harry if maybe it wasn't a hand-rolled cigarette, but Harry was positive. I went down and confronted Moe. He admitted he had been smoking marijuana. I felt betrayed, and I experienced one of the dangers of becoming more personal with students. For several weeks I resented my favorite students, who had let this happen. I was really hurt; my trust had been betrayed by students I respected the most. That hurt was much worse than my fear parents or the school administration would find out, although that worried me too. Sometimes I think we should have packed up and left the camp at that moment, even though that would have punished the non-guilty students and have created too big a scene for something so commonplace among kids as smoking a joint. We did leave the next morning with due sullenness on my part.

Several years later, one of those still-favorite former students tried to explain to me the perspective they had had as adolescents.

"We knew he shouldn't have been smoking, but we couldn't stop him. Besides, you were a teacher. You were important. Nothing could happen to you."

Once again, I had deserved an F for not understanding my liabilities.

Honor and betrayal are fixtures in what it means to be a teacher.

11

At Risk

What emerges from the (study) is a sense that teachers are underpaid and under appreciated. Together with school administrators . . . they are legally and often physically vulnerable.

—Eugene Provenzo Jr.

Teaching is not a lost art, but the regard for it is a lost tradition.

—Jacques Barzun

Teachers are vulnerable. The vignettes and stories in this chapter emphasize the dramatic ways in which teachers are so especially vulnerable. This is also a convenient place to address the issue of teacher unions. The decision a teacher makes about whether to join a union, and if yes, which union, helps define a teacher's specific educational identity. At some time or another most, if not all of us teachers would have preferred the independent role of "the professional." As with doctors and lawyers, a professional association would have been fine.

But on the whole we are far too vulnerable far too often to rely on a loose-knit organization of working professionals. While my experience has been that the preponderance of school board members, administrators, department chairs, parents, and students are well-meaning people, there are plenty of exceptions that add peril to the lives of teachers.

There's a saying that no good deed goes unpunished. A school board member once kept a secret file on me because I had not hired a favored,

if undependable, teacher for summer school. A district curriculum supervisor tried to have me fired for not correcting spelling and grammar on a
creative writing assignment. A principal let a probationary teacher who I
considered most effective go because of a messy classroom. A vice principal tried to make me flunk a student I had never had in a class. A department chair that I had would go on tirades and then, sometimes, break
down into uncontrollable tears. As suggested in chapter 2, all teachers are
faced with job conditions that without some checks and balances would
become truly unworkable. There are teacher contracts about class sizes
because so many times principals were without conscience on how many
students they'd allow in a classroom. Many school board members don't
know, and many school administrators have forgotten, what the minimal
wage is to subsist as a school teacher. Most of us, especially as we get
older, really do need a bathroom break. We aren't always right, but we really do need grievance procedures to protect our rights without having to
rely on persuasion, or the courts.

Somehow the media tends to represent unions as the reason we have
poor teachers. I absolutely know from firsthand experience and research
that school administrators are overworked. But if teacher quality was
treated as the priority it should be, in most states poor teachers could be
screened out of teaching by evaluating them in the first two years they are
at school. Even then, though, it is a scary proposition because there are
enough poor administrators more interested in blind obedience than effective teaching.

So, we have teacher unions, and even teachers who do not join are
given some amount of protection by the unions. Salaries do not necessarily keep up with jobs that require comparable education, nor with infla-
tion, but they could be worse. States like California have ridiculously high
average class sizes, but it could be worse. Administrators, parents, and
students occasionally do outrageous things, and we have grievance procedures. We feel vulnerable in so many ways that we are thankful for organized labor.

As we individually search out what it means to be a teacher, we are generally employed in a position that has an inherent identity crisis: professional in the classroom, blue collar outside the classroom. Most all of us
handle this ambivalence very nicely, thank you. But in this chapter on
teacher vulnerability it is the place to appreciate what protection organi-

zations like the National Education Association (NEA) and the American Federation of Teachers (AFT) are able to provide.

Teachers are vulnerable. Maybe 99 percent of the time we are perfectly safe, but we are always aware of being at risk. Students can erupt into violence; students' relatives can come to school with a grievance; outsiders can at anytime put anyone on school grounds at risk for any number of reasons. The stories in the newspapers about violence on campuses are newsworthy because they are exceptions to the routine. But the reality for every teacher is that the potential for danger is lurking just around the corner.

My stories present situations that are perhaps more dramatic than those most teachers have actually encountered. Yet some teachers have experienced events dramatically worse. The stories here reflect an increasing sense of personal danger, but I end the chapter with a story about professional danger. Any treatment of what it means to be a teacher must necessarily deal with the many ways in which teachers are so potentially vulnerable.

RIOT

Near the beginning of my first year as a teacher we had a full school riot. In college, we had all-school dances, but those matched none of the excitement of an all-school riot. Twenty-three hundred kids were running hysterically through the corridors yelling and screaming and fighting.

It started with a bomb threat. This resulted in a fire drill and twenty-three hundred students standing around in the hot sun. When the riot was over I wrote the following:

Damn kids. Why did they have to go and start a riot? What happened? No one seems sure. The bomb scare, taking our classes out to the football field, the heat, the disorganization, the tempers. The conflagration in the quad while we were returning to classes. A fight. It was quickly broken up, but there were still the crowds, and the crowds had nowhere to go. The first fight seemed over, but everyone was still edgy and no one seemed to have anywhere else they wanted to go. Then all Hell broke loose. You can't even remember exactly what happened next for sure. You were trying to break up the crowd near your classroom when there was a sudden surge of students toward the circular Art Building in the middle of the quad. Crowds usually moved toward fights. The crowd cut you off but you thought you should get to that center of trouble. You knew you shouldn't run and make things seem dramatic, but you did. You ran around the circular Art Building so that you could get into it. Mrs. Manicotti, the Librarian, told you to stay out, you might get hurt, it wasn't worth it, there was only so much the teachers had to do. There wasn't, however, any question, but that you would go. You could see it was looking tight for teachers Montgomery Steadfast and Juan Mendoza on the runway into the Art Building. The fight and the crowd had cornered them. They were trying to break up the groups in the quad by putting some of the students into the Art Building. Their efforts were only partially effective. You pulled a kid off Mr. Mendoza's back. The student's eyes were glazed. You thought his glassy blue eyes betrayed him as being on drugs. Maybe it was adrenaline. Where did you go from there and what did you do? It is still unclear. All you remember is going from group to group telling people to be calm and get out of the quad. You traveled from one end of campus to the other and back again. Just as the riot seemed to quell, it burst out again somewhere else.

There were just too many people and not enough faculty members. Several times you wondered if the police weren't going to be called to help. You had heard that was what usually happened. For awhile, it didn't seem like the riot would ever end. You remember Denny Boyd, one of your students. When you walked past him, he'd raise his hands toward other students and yell, "Stop this." Then over your shoulder, after he thought you had passed, he'd swing at someone or yell, "Get him!" The black kids were for the most part staying out of the riot. And the white kids were nowhere to be seen. At first, it was the Chicano guys, then it was mixed groups, black and brown, and then at the end it was mostly hysterical girls. One black girl had fainted. When she came to, she ran wildly, anywhere. She grabbed the first Chicana she could and took one swing. They both went down; Montgomery got there first. He held one girl and tried to hold off the other. You got there in time to stop a black student from taking a swing at Montgomery from behind. The student wasn't emotional, he just apparently wanted to take a swing. You also stopped another student from hitting Montgomery from behind with a small tree that the student had pulled up by its roots.

The action then surged toward the other end of campus. You went down there just as a group was about to break into a classroom. Hank Garfield, the Basketball Coach, was down there. One tall kid (black or Chicano?) seemed to be trying to take charge. For a moment, the group listened. He seemed at first to be advocating a departure, so you hoped he was a positive leader. You looked at Garfield, and both of you seemed to think at the same time—let him talk—maybe he can help. Then both of your visible disappointment showed at the same time when he cursed, "We can get them tonight." At least the crowd dispersed some then and you walked quickly back toward the office. There was a black girl still down and apparently needing a stretcher. She had been hit hard in the stomach and was still lying out in the quad. You went and got the stretcher. Gee, there were a lot of kids in the office. You hoped the situation in the office would not become uncomfortable. You helped the girl on the stretcher, but it was impossible to keep her there. Her sister was sobbing hysterically and trying to pull her from the stretcher. The nurse who was with you talked a black male student into stopping the girl's sister from interfering. She seemed panicked, so you held the hand of the girl on the stretcher to comfort her. You cringed to think that she might detest the aid of a white man in this situation. You thought, why can't I be like a chameleon and change my color for the moment.

Another incident with the stretcher was almost comical. You and three other male teachers tried to carry a hysterical female student to the office on the stretcher. She had been apparently unconscious when you first put her on the stretcher. She aroused, became immediately hysterical and flailed herself off the stretcher, only apparently to pass out again. The four of you picked her up again, put her on the stretcher, only to have her arouse and fling herself off again. This happened three times before you were able to get her to the office.

You couldn't understand why the police hadn't helped, but it was finally over. Apparently the riot lasted about an hour, but it seemed much longer. The groups were dispersed. You were glad to find out that you weren't a coward and you were almost happy because everything had finally ended and no one had been hurt seriously. You have had numerous reactions since, including your present reflective mood. Your immediate response had been to smile. You had passed the test. Everyone had done their job and a tragic disaster had been avoided. You were thankful—no one had died, especially yourself. You felt very uneasy during the subsequent faculty meeting because there seemed to be a lot more entering into the discussion than the problem at hand. Each person seemed to be using the trouble for his/her own platform. Emotion was still high and the faculty needed time to sort out what had happened. The faculty had been in conference virtually since the riot and had not had time to collect itself.

The faculty seemed to primarily blame the School Superintendent, Hank Rossellini, for the riot. You had the feeling that each faculty member was standing up and grinding old axes you were unfamiliar with. There seemed to be a great confusion about how the whole situation had developed and it bothered you that none of the people you had helped, who had been out in the thick of things, were saying anything. A PE teacher expressed his interpretation of the cause of the riot. The black "boys," he said, had been dating Mexican girls on campus. The Mexican boys needed to demonstrate their masculinity, but not against the blacks who tended to be bigger, so they fought each other. The insecure black girls, needing to gain the attention of the black boys back — got it through the rioting. It was a curious interpretation. You didn't know what to think about the problems of color, which obviously had had something to do with the riot. There may be real racial problems in the school, but they cannot just be written off as a difference in the color of skins. Although the newspapers described the conflict as having been between blacks and browns, you had seen more rival brown students fighting each other. You wondered about the underlying causes and heard no satisfactory explanation in the faculty meetings.

Another problem you became concerned about was the difference between reality and the verbalization of reality. You were concerned that the reality of the riot was being formed by the discussion, not from the hour in the halls. It seemed a real problem that the verbalization held precedence over the actual incidents.

Well, those seemed to be your overriding concerns. But there was one other. You wrote it down earlier at home because you couldn't keep your mind off Fields High School: "I almost feel glad because it seems that now, maybe now, we can strip away the facade and get down to the essence, what these kids think, what they know and how we can communicate." You weren't ashamed or afraid of your students. So many tried to help. Even many of the students you couldn't "excuse" for their acts were acting out of what you considered misguided loyalty. That so much could happen without anyone being seriously hurt indicated the conflicts might not be as deep as feared. People could easily have been seriously hurt, but weren't. The troublemakers were still a very small percentage. Maybe we can make some more drastic changes to improve the school and some good can come out of the riot.

I would really like to censor a word the PE Coach used. It reflected a lack of sensitivity I also started teaching with. I have not used the word "boy" since that time. It is taboo, an emotionally charged, trigger word. Chicano and black "young men." The term "boy" may be a perfectly acceptable white-middle-class word for a male child, but the history of slavery is still too recent for everyone to forget the degrading use of the word "boy" for any black male regardless of age.

Following the riot, the school was closed down for three days not to start again until the following Monday. The teachers came and started exciting rumors. One of the best was that the Black Panthers were being bussed down from Oakland to help their black brothers in case of further trouble. I was confident of one thing, if the Panthers were coming, they were not going to come down in a bus. Can you imagine a bus of gun toting Black Panthers riding together down the freeway to San Juan from Oakland without causing some suspicion that would hamper their chances of ever making it to San Jose?

One of the janitors started another rumor that caused even more concern. He theorized that the kids would hide guns on the roof. The longer we met, the greater the loss of perspective. Fortunately, we had a superintendent that lent us his. He came down and gave us an inspirational speech full of clichés and double-talk and when he got down to his choking conclusion, he bade us farewell and God Bless. Thanks Hank. And then Monday arrived without incident. Control was reestablished. Police were on campus, and since there was no more violence, "obviously" the necessary changes had been made. So that was that.

SMOKING

Working late after a particularly frustrating day, I walked out of my room into a gang of about twelve young men standing around smoking. There are strong social expectations in such a school situation at Fields High. If the students will hide their cigarettes, the teacher will usually ignore them. As I passed, a student blew cigarette smoke into my face. I did what I recommend never doing. I took a stance and felt then bound by it too specifically. I told the student to put out his cigarette. He passed it to a friend. I wanted the original student to put out his cigarette with no alternative solution possible. Here I am standing next to twelve—count 'em—twelve guys, any one of whom could do me in, with no other teacher or student in sight. Fields High had already proven to be precarious. Did I ignore the scene and walk on? Of course not.

"OK, give me the cigarette," I said. Now I was really committed. So that authority can maintain itself, it insists on winning every encounter. I was determined that I, as authority, would not yield to these students' delinquency in any way.

General Bowden, a "liaison" man, a guy hired to serve as an intermediary between the school staff and students and their families, made the mistake of coming out of his office door about this time. General was the same color as the students, and he begged off and retreated into his room. It was clearly my problem. I continued to polarize the situation. The student put out the cigarette, but I had now asked for the cigarette, and since I was the authority, I had to see that my directions were followed precisely. I really chewed the guys out and eventually the vice principal came down and ran them off campus. I had thought I had done the right thing, but it didn't feel right. The next morning in the front office when I was greeted as a hero who had taken on an entire gang of the enemy, I took no pride. I had handled the situation poorly. I should have stopped the smoking, but I shouldn't have taken the situation personally. In fact, it turned out that many in this group were gang members from the neighborhood, not students. I had undoubtedly underestimated the potential peril.

Timothy

Probably the greatest personal danger I ever faced was while working at an inner-city "youth house." Even though this was not an official school, the particular situation I faced could happen to any teacher. This is what I wrote that same night about what happened:

I'm not really sure if I'll remember more now that it's fresh or later when I've had a chance to think about it. It's really difficult to know if this was rather ordinary or something I will look back on as having great significance.

It started off wrong when Paul Anderson (the director of Cairo Youth Academy) got sick and could not go to the bank to get the kids' checks cashed. Also, when Paul got sick, I had to take over the leather craft class.

I was out talking to some of the girls when Timothy first came up. He was obviously very loaded and obviously recovering from a recent fight. His left eye was sealed shut. He "jived" a bit with the girls and the first thing I remember him saying was, "I'm seeing pretty good now." He said it with a laugh. The next thing significant enough to remember was his asking me if I had any money.

"You got any money?"

"Nah, at least not much."

Timothy then started to reach into my front left pocket. I had my hands in my jacket pockets so I gently pushed his hand away from my pocket.

"Don't you push my hand away. I'll cut you."

"I wish you wouldn't," and I actually think I said it rather matter-of-factly.

"If I reach in your pocket, you just let me. If I want your money, you just ask me how much."

Mumble, mumble, on my part.

"I'll cut your tongue out."

"I wish you wouldn't."

"I can whip you."

"I'm sure you can."

During this fascinating conversation, Timothy pulled out his knife. But he also stumbled. I figured that even though he was very loaded on "red devils," he could slice me up pretty quick if he really did fight me. But I knew that I wouldn't fight him in any circumstances. Later I was to tell him I wouldn't want to do anything to hurt him, and that that didn't mean I could handle him in a fight.

The red devils must have broken his concentration because he started talking to the girls some then and this potential confrontation passed on by. After he talked to Sancho some, they both went into the front room where the leather shop was being run. I was responsible so I followed Timothy on in. There was a crowd at the door and I figured that could be a "bummer," but I was able to squeeze on in and around the leather working table. Buford and Paul (not the director) were jiving with Timothy. Timothy mentioned that if the other dude had beat him in the fight that Timothy wouldn't still be walking around. He also confessed that he had been hurt pretty good since he was more loaded than the other cat.

The topic of conversation stayed around what Timothy would do to that cat next time he saw him, how he was loaded, about his eye, and about how tough he was. Again, the fact that he was loaded had a lot to do with the stream of the conversation. I tried to avoid looking directly at Timothy because his encounters seemed to be dependent upon whom Timothy seemed challenged by. I just wanted to make sure things didn't get really out of hand.

Timothy started messing with Paul with the knife. Paul got out his razor blade and assured Timothy that he didn't want him cutting him with that knife. Timothy started to cut him. Paul lunged away from him.

"Don't be doing that nigger," Paul demanded.

"You afraid of getting cut?" Timothy challenged.

"I don't want to be scratched up like you," Paul said.

"Why, you can't take it?" Timothy asked.

"No, man, I don't want none of them marks like yours," Paul countered.

Timothy started taking off his coat. All the many, many people in the room started moving back real quick like so I figured something must be coming. In the movies the cat takes off his coat for a fight. But then this didn't seem exactly like the movies.

Sure enough it wasn't. Timothy didn't take the knife to anyone. He took it to himself. He slashed his arm. His own arm. And it obviously was not the first time. There were many scars on that left arm. Sancho grabbed Timothy's arm. "Aw, it isn't even bleeding yet." It wasn't bleeding only because the knife wasn't very sharp. Timothy indicated to the watching masses that it didn't even hurt.

Somewhere in the midst of this same conversation Timothy challenged Paul to do the same thing. Paul again confided in Timothy that he didn't want to cut himself. "I don't want to hurt my delicate skin."

The comic interplay along with all this was slightly confusing to me. Although Timothy was taking issue with some challenges from some of the others about his behavior, he was sharing some of Buford's jokes about his being loaded now too, so how was he going to take care of that cat he had been in a fight with now if he couldn't then.

Somewhere during all this I stood up. It had been obvious to me that I wasn't going to throw Timothy out of the class. And besides that Buford and Paul had been handling the situation rather masterfully. Buford didn't like Timothy cutting himself and saved me the necessity of moving toward Timothy to make him put the knife away. Timothy turned the knife toward Buford. I think Buford asked him, "Now why do you want to do that?"

Buford then added, "Okay, we're going to lock up. Everyone get on out. Where's the keys?"

Look out. Guess who had the keys. And remember, Timothy's favorite line had been, "I'll cut your tongue out." I was interested in where he had gotten that particular syntax. During this time I discovered it went with, "I'll cut out your tongue, like I did that dog down the street." Fine.

"Here's the keys Buford." What a man Gose. What bravery.

"Don't you go telling me what to do." Timothy was talking to me. My time had come to be included with the continuing discussion with Timothy.

"I'm not telling you to do anything. Buford asked for the keys," I responded. Thank God for Buford.

"I'll cut your tongue out," Timothy told me.

Paul and Buford and some others came to my defense. I was proud though unable to take proper notice of who all had chimed in. "Mike ain't never done nothing to you."

It was about this time that I assured Timothy that he was a man and I wasn't trying to tell him nothing.

It was also during this time that Timothy stabbed at Buford. That got more people moving out the door. The exact proceedings are difficult to recall. I am quite sure though that Timothy offered to cut Buford, Paul, and myself and that he had demonstrated this interest by slashing himself and stabbing at Buford. I really think we could have gotten Timothy on out the door, but at this point someone had gone and gotten Paul (Anderson, the director). It struck me as unusual that I hadn't even thought about going to get Paul. This thought struck me at that very moment but I had kind of figured it was my thing to work out. If I couldn't pass that test, I might as well hang it up. In any instance, Paul got Timothy on out the door and toward the front gate by asking him to just tell him what was going on.

I thought about staying on back considering the possibility that being out there might provoke Timothy again. But I wasn't about to do anything looking like I was hiding. I figured that would really be worse in the long run. So I went out and leaned against the fence next to Paul Anderson and just watched what was going down.

During this time the girls expressed surprise that I hadn't tangled with Timothy. I think it was Mookie who asked if I wouldn't "be ashamed to be beaten by a Negro." I think they were really surprised that I hadn't reacted to Timothy by fighting.

"What good would that have done?" I asked.

"He wouldn't be fighting," someone said of me.

"Did anyone fight? Did anyone get hurt?" I had been successful so far in my own eyes.

"But weren't you afraid?" Mookie asked.

"I don't seem to have sense enough to be afraid," I responded.

"Shoot, they'll beat down on someone for being the wrong color when they're loaded," I was warned.

No one had to add that I was definitely the wrong color. Some time passed here that I don't remember clearly until Timothy came back. First he wanted to borrow a dollar from Paul (the director). Paul told him he didn't have any money. Then Timothy came to me.

"You got any money?" he asked.

I would not lie. I might try to con someone and say my principles are strictly against lying (and they usually are). But I think I had already thought it would be much worse for me to get caught lying to Timothy.

"Yeah, I got a little bit of money," I said.

"Lend me a dollar."

"I'm not sure I should."

"Sure you should. I'll pay you back."

"I'm sure you will."

"Really, I'll pay you back."

"I believe you."

Some of the others standing around were saying to not give him the dollar and that he wouldn't pay me back. I think Timothy must have been more conscious of that than I was.

"Look, if I lent you a dollar in your condition, would it be helping you or hurting you?" I wanted to know.

"It'd be helping me."

"Are you sure? How?"

"Yeah, I need to go buy me a couple half gallons of milk to get my high down."

"Okay, I'm going to lend you a dollar."

Numerous of the guys were advising me against it. I had looked at Paul a little earlier but got no sign about what to do so I was strictly on my own judgment. I knew that if Timothy thought he was suckering me now I'd be in for a lot of shakedowns later. "I'll loan you the dollar but I want you to know this: I'm not giving it to you because I'm afraid of you, and I don't want you to think that because I gave you a dollar this time you can shake me down later. I'm giving you this dollar because you said you need it."

"I really need it. I need to get this high down. I'll pay you back. I'll pay you back tonight if my friends show up, and if they don't I'll pay you tomorrow, and if you aren't here, I'll give it to Paul."

"I believe you."

"Really I will."

"Remember, I'm giving it to you because you told me you needed it to help yourself."

"Man to man. I need that dollar," Timothy said earnestly.

"Okay." He gave me the grip and thanked me. Okay.

Even Paul Anderson said when a guy is loaded like that you should just tell him you don't have any money.

"I didn't want to lie to him, Paul," I said in defense of myself. And the guys chimed in with more "you shouldn't have done its." I proclaimed that I'd risk a dollar on any one of you guys. The other Paul promptly pretended to be loaded.

I told him, "Shoot, I'll just whoop yer head," and playfully pushed him down on the sidewalk. I realized the irony that I would risk the money with the fighter and turn around and play fight with the guy who could have probably used a dollar also. It really wasn't a matter of dollars and cents. I really felt it was a matter of meeting pressing human needs. Even my own.

"We'll see." I was optimistic Timothy would pay me back. And to a man no one thought I would get that dollar back. I'm always a bit rebellious, so I took a wait-and-see attitude. I didn't have time to second guess myself. Timothy's friends showed up in a car. Timothy went to the car. Then here came Timothy. "Thanks man." Timothy handed me the dollar.

"Anytime." I stuffed it in my pocket and glanced around at the unbelieving group of doubting Thomases. I had a funny feeling I might be participating in a miracle, but I acted like it was expected. I looked at Buford and gave him one of those didn't I tell you looks. There were really some surprised faces. I didn't make a big deal about it. I just let it ride. Buford said, "It sure was a surprise."

I figured there was a message, but I figured this was kind of like a parable come to life and I just let the story stand for itself.

P.S. Timothy is now doing life in prison for a series of kidnaps and murders.

POTENTIAL TROUBLE

There is always the potential for trouble around a school.

Item: I believe I once forestalled a race riot at our high school. Officials lost control of the basketball game. Sunset Landing students yelled "Jungle bunny," "nigger," "coon," at the visiting team, especially their cheerleaders, much to my chagrin. My inner-city experience paid off as I, by myself, ordered students in, out, and around and got our opponents successfully to their bus. (Which was then "rocked" on the way home after it had left campus. Fortunately, no one was injured.)

Item: The bus ahead of me, on a bus trip after a night football game at a rival high school, was rocked and one of our students got glass fragments in her eye. I got out and walked through a hostile crowd to call police for assistance. That first bus driver panicked and left to another barrage of rocks. Fortunately the girl was okay.

Quentin

During one school year, my latent cautiousness (and paranoia) about how close teachers always are to extremely serious situations was validated. A teacher at Middlemarch Continuation School was forced out of his job for something he most probably did not do. Who knows what evil lurks in the hearts of men?

To my mind, there is something inherently inequitable about an all-Anglo staff teaching students of Mexican and black backgrounds. We had, quote-unquote, not been able to find qualified minority teachers. Taking my "white man's burden" upon myself, I visited the Occidental College Placement Center. They felt they might have some possible "minority" candidates for us. I did no screening or recommendation of those candidates, but for one reason or another, the principal hired a candidate from that group. The principal was very proud of getting two minorities for the price of one. He hired a Spanish-speaking, black Puerto Rican.

It wasn't clear in my mind that we had solved our problem of students having a staff member closer to their own identities to model themselves after. Truthfully, because he was Puerto Rican, neither his black nor Spanish experiences were representative of the black or Chicano students in our classes. We just had one more teacher who students might not identify with, but who might or might not nonetheless be an effective teacher.

Quentin had some problems. His manner and manners, were, well, different. And for all our cultural diversity, most of us have not, as a group of people, learned to appreciate that diversity. The high school kids were all used to coping with white America and white teachers; they couldn't figure Quentin out. He was highly intellectual, and somewhat aggressive and confrontive, forward. He was very dark-skinned and had an unusual accent, and perhaps a trace of a lisp. He was not readily accepted. The black kids were suspicious of his Spanish and the Spanish kids of his blackness. And the "unenlightened" white kids didn't like him for both reasons.

But Quentin was on the staff, and Bart and I probably knew him best because of our (choose one) (a) "racial tolerance," (b) curiosity, (c) respect for his intellect. But to say we knew him best did not mean we knew him well. I still believe most employment decisions that discriminate racially are not made to so much exclude someone as to include someone closest to one's own, usually ethnocentric, standards. Like it or not, there are likely to be barriers between peoples of very different life experiences. As "enlightened" and "progressive" as Bart and I considered ourselves to be, there were certain barriers between us and Quentin—even a distrust— because of certain unknowns about him, even though we had been and continued to be very supportive of his teaching. Still, we could not assume he was "one of us," in terms of how he was likely to act. I admit to these shortcomings to also suggest the probable limits other, less "enlightened" and "progressive," teachers would have in support of Quentin. As long as nothing "happened," it really didn't matter. But something did happen, something potentially very serious.

A seventeen-year-old white male student (described cynically by another teacher as "rich white trash") accused Quentin of having propositioned him sexually. There were no witnesses.

Bart and I agreed, Quentin couldn't have done that. Could he? (We thought, even if he was homosexual—and he was married, which tended to indicate otherwise—he couldn't be that stupid. Could he?) The implications of a public hearing on the matter were staggering. Imagine the community, split by a freeway, with rich white on one side, Chicano and black on the other. Imagine a community in the early 1970s that contained black berets, brown berets, John Birch members, and Ku Klux Klan members. Imagine trying a Spanish-speaking black Puerto Rican about sexual conduct. Imagine the hostility and potential for violence.

Bart and I were 99.9 percent sure Quentin was innocent of the allegation. Clearly a court would have to exonerate him because of the lack of evidence. But, oh my, what potential trouble lurked in the meantime.

Quentin, a very intelligent person, sized up the opposition and the consequences of winning (because we felt he couldn't "lose" a court case) and resigned. Neither Bart nor I tried to change his mind. Quentin had a better appreciation of the enormity of the situation that we did.

Quentin was helpless; Quentin was exceedingly vulnerable; Quentin was black in white America. An unstable seventeen-year-old blond male was able to cost Quentin his job. It was reminiscent of Harper Lee's portrayal of how the Ewells (in the Maycomb County of *To Kill a Mockingbird*) cost Tom Robinson his life through a falsely alleged seduction. Perhaps the slow but continued progress of America in the years since the time in which *To Kill a Mockingbird* was set was that Quentin escaped with his life, if not his job. I feel badly to still reaffirm that Quentin probably did take the expedient course of action. Justice was not possible.

It may be to a lesser degree than for soldiers, policemen, and firemen, but teachers are always vulnerable and at risk. And it unsettles us a bit more than we like to admit.

12

Joys of Teaching

My joy in learning is partly that it enables me to teach.

—Seneca

One of the greatest satisfactions of teaching, in my own belief, is the ever-present possibility of "taking the imagination by surprise"—our own imagination or that of the children in our midst.

—Jonathan Kozol

And we would all recognize for an instant the foolishness and absurdity of our ways through the world and feel the impact of the great, occasional and accidental joy which would be our only reward along those paths.

—James Herndon

Although the times cannot be planned, and tend to be unexpected, there are great and particular joys that come with teaching. These joys are the primary rewards of our chosen profession. These are the times when we get involved in the creative process and produce something original ourselves, when we actually make a difference for a student or something out of the ordinary happens. It's when we find just the right thing to do for or with an exasperating student. These tend to be the stories that keep us going, that are our delight.

GETTING HAPPY

My friend, Professor David Holmes, calls it "getting happy." There are those moments, infrequent, but too often to be called rare, when a teacher simply steps outside of the time-space continuum and experiences a sliver of eternity. All systems are go. Every student is involved, every beat is precious, time is immaterial. You simply step outside of yourself. The feeling is not unique to teaching; it is inspired. Yet in teaching, the spirit is breathed into the classroom. You didn't create it, but you are a part of it. You are caught up, animated, made vital. Teacher and students are together. Perhaps touched by an angel, the spirit soars.

Sometimes these moments occur when we ourselves get involved with our students in a creative enterprise.

Making Films

Making films was fun, if not educational. Intuitively, it seemed like a legitimate means of self-expression, and I certainly could justify it educationally to anyone who challenged me. But I never did worry too much about exactly how it fit into the English curriculum. Alfredo Sax did an excellent film, about variations on a theme. Alfredo took the camera and filmed legs, all kinds of legs: shapely legs, bandy legs, stocky legs, legs that crossed, legs that jumped, hairy legs, knobby knees. The film had great focus. The students loved it, too, so I gave Alfredo an A. Generous of me, huh?

I did a film, too. It was a *Mission Impossible* film, and the students helped me with it. The mission was to expose my friend, Montgomery, who was also in the English Department and who was, according to the plot line, making his students work too hard. In the film, I arrived in my sports car (I had bought an Opel GT, which looked like a baby Corvette, got me a lot of early attention, and turned out to be a terrible car). I got out, wearing my topcoat and English hat, and walked to the food machines, where I put in a quarter and took out a tape recorder. The tone was set when, in five seconds, I went up in smoke instead of the tape recording, as happens in the TV series. The *Mission Impossible* plan was to drive Mr. Steadfast crazy. He showed up to class by bounding into the picture wearing a cape and with an "S" on his chest. We had three plans. First, all his students would be in class one second and disappear the next (which was easily accomplished by holding the camera still and stopping and starting the film). Next, one of his students would keep appearing all over the class instantaneously. By this time, Montgomery was acting as if he was going crazy. Meanwhile, one of the students (who had devised a fancy-looking electrical gadget in electric shop) pushed a button on his machine that made the clock go extra fast; the bell rang and when Montgomery tried to keep the students from running out the door, they trampled him. Defeated, Montgomery walked down to the faculty bathroom and flushed himself down the toilet. Maybe it wasn't a great film, but it was fun. And being active in the same learning environment as the students may have been the greatest lesson I ever "taught," though I only barely sensed the full importance of "modeling" at that time. Through such projects learning was taking place.

Buck, Timmy, Leroy, and group did the finest film. The students asked to see it over and over again. To me, the best part of the project was that blacks, whites, and browns worked together toward a common goal. It is shocking how infrequently that happens, even at an integrated school. Most of the work in a comprehensive high school is individual, and what rare small-group work there is often forced or insignificant. These guys really did a job, making full use of their own racial differences.

Their film opened on a group of white and brown students rolling a joint (i.e., a marijuana cigarette) out in back of school. The local narc, played by teacher Moe Rizzuto, saw them and tried to catch them with the goods. The students hid the "grass" in their belts at the small of their backs. (Which was also a favorite place for hiding squirt guns.) Moe frisked them, but could not find the stuff, so he threw up his hands and left. The students immediately went back to rolling their joint and smoking it, passing it around amongst themselves.

All was going well until a group of black students, who were drinking a bottle of wine as they walked down the street "sharing the good news," spotted the smokers and leapt the fence to get in on the pot smoking. Timmy Cliff was the first on the scene and the white guys started pushing him around. Things started getting rowdy and a fight erupted. When Timmy was pushed down, he pulled out a knife that (proving a little luck does not hurt good planning) glinted in the sun. He stabbed Marshall. The students then ran as the narc (Moe Rizzuto) ran back into the scene. As he watched the students run, he picked up the dropped joint, and as the camera panned away, Moe "toked up."

The movie had all the components of a popular film, save sex. There was violence and drugs and esprit de corps and racial conflict. The students asked to see the film almost every day for the rest of the year. And sometimes I showed it again, usually when I myself was anxious to see it just one more time.

Even "remembered joy" brightens a day.

Herbert

If you want to get some really fine discussion or writing, ask kids what the most embarrassing thing that ever happened to them in school was. If you can get them to write or talk about this, it really helps ease some of the uneasiness that may have been kept as secret as possible for years.

I introduced the subject of embarrassing moments by reminiscing on two of my own particularly embarrassing encounters. The first I mentioned was when I was in eighth grade. I asked my B-period snack group of fellow students rather loudly, "Who likes Old Lady Sajak?"

As it turned out Old Lady Sajak was standing right behind me.

The second occasion I mentioned was in eleventh grade. Acting childishly at a fire drill, I was selected to take the drill attendance to the office. I took off running as fast as I could run, still acting childishly. The class was urging me on with, "Go, Gose, go." I hit a dip in the pavement and did a complete summersault in the air. My pen cracked in midair and it tore the side of my pants out. I limped off to derisive laughing.

I'm kind of embarrassed to repeat the most embarrassing story told by a student. A tall, well-built kid named Herb admitted to a story I do not think I, as a student, would have ever mentioned, regardless of the assignment. Herb was in the eighth-grade Christmas play. They were doing *The Night before Christmas* and Herb was wearing his pajamas. Actually he was wearing his nightshirt, the nightshirt that he always wore to bed at his own house, and he did not even think about wearing underwear beneath them. You guessed it. When it came time for Herb to "open the shutters and throw up the sash," his nightshirt got caught and Herb exposed himself to the entire eighth-grade class.

As an eighth-grader he probably should have changed schools, if not states. But it was a great story for everyone else.

June

All of our stories as teachers are not necessarily about students. The school was a forum in which we could all share our creative exploits. June Frampton was a superlative mimic of such characters as Lily Tomlin's Edith Ann, President Nixon, and each of us behind our backs. She was a VISTA University Year for ACTION aide to our high school program. One day she put on a bravura performance recapitulating the role of Paul Newman in *Cool Hand Luke:* she ate two dozen hard-boiled eggs in a single hour.

The idea began innocently enough with a "great moments in cinema" discussion that ran well past the end of the regular school day. The consensus of our group was that Newman's eating of fifty eggs in an hour in *Cool Hand Luke* was the greatest moment in cinema history. I mentioned to the group that contests had been run in honor of Cool Hand Luke's feat and someone (I thought a three-hundred-pound Texan) had set a real record of forty-two eggs in an hour, eight under Luke's record in the movie.

Very matter of factly, June, a slender, one-hundred-pound, droll daredevil told our group, (which now, excepting June, consisted only of males), "I can eat twenty-four eggs in an hour."

Everyone was incredulous. Much like in the movie, everyone started laying bets, although not much money passed hands because no one thought she would or could do it.

It was a case study of creative problem solving. Students pooled their money to buy the eggs, and one of the students who had a car instead of a motorcycle went off to the store. It was determined that we'd boil the water for the eggs on the hot plate we usually reserved for the coffeepot. Another student went in successful pursuit of a vat in which to boil them. June was definite: she expected hard-boiled, not soft-boiled eggs.

'Twas a memorable hour. June consumed eighteen eggs in the first thirty minutes, surprisingly easily. The last six went down with much greater difficulty amidst a heated argument about whether she could "wet her whistle" or not. With five minutes left, she still had three eggs to go. I judiciously looked for and found a leakproof wastebasket should she throw up.

Then she had one egg and one minute left. Her face was ashen. The final imbroglio was whether any remnants of albumen on her palate would defeat her gallant effort. The argument was moot. Roger insisted on feeling inside her cheeks, but she had cleanly downed them all. She won. We were all convinced we'd seen a piece of history. The incident always helped us keep our other accomplishments in perspective.

The depth of any of our education seems more related to the small, incremental, largely forgotten moments we experience working through the curriculum. The joys are usually in the unpredicted, unexpected, exceptional moments along the way.

Magnum of Champagne

Schools also provide opportunities for a camaraderie I cherish. Mark Mc-Donald and I went to a Title IV-C conference in San Diego. The Title IV Program at least theoretically is a well-conceived program. Through it, some prospectively valuable programs are funded and the best of those programs are determined to be "model" programs that other schools can obtain funding to adopt or adapt. On the basis of Mark's and my application (and the school district's support) we received a Title IV-C grant. Written into the grant, actually preliminarily written into the proposal application itself, was a mandatory $400 budget line for this Title IV-C conference. You lost that money if you didn't go to the conference and spend it all. Mark and I wouldn't have missed such an opportunity. We weren't about to lose the $400 back to the Feds. And besides, we had friends who lived in San Diego so we could visit them as well. The trick was to go and spend no more or less than the $400.

We rented a car while there, which might have been unnecessary except we were able to avoid the greater expense of staying in a hotel by staying with friends. So even after airfare, we stayed within the grant's $400. However, on the last day of the conference it was apparent we would be spending a few dollars less than the entire $400 if we didn't think of something. We were determined to spend every one of those dollars. After all, we paid our income taxes to Uncle Sam and we wanted to help him spend some of that money. So we decided to skip out on the lunch at the conference and go to lunch at Anthony's Fish Grotto (to my mind one of the best restaurants in San Diego). We ordered and feasted on abalone steaks (which were outrageously priced but delectable) and quaffed them down with a magnum of fine champagne.

There's a name for the kind of grins we exhibited as we moseyed on back to the fort for the remainder of the conference day. Perhaps you know it. This was a memorable event. Mark and I recognized for an instant the foolishness of our ways through the world and the joys of its unplanned rewards.

Creative Spurt

Sometimes the students inspire the teacher to unexpected creative outbursts. I thoroughly enjoyed how much my students enjoyed this creation of mine while I was teaching them tenth-grade English.

Ode to My Children from a Resolute Parent

I told you so,
but you wouldn't listen.
You said, "I know,"
but you really didn't.

Your music's too loud
In fact it's absurd.
When I turn around
you flip me the bird.

Comb your hair.
I think you smell.
You better be good
or you're going to hell.

Your friends are wild,
they must drink booze.
Tuck in your shirt
and polish your shoes.

Be in by ten
and don't be late
If you are,
it'll be a mistake.

Mind your manners,
stay on your toes.
Be sure to be good,
don't pick your nose.

Be sure to obey,
don't pick your pimples.
Stay away
from girls with dimples.

Don't go far.
It's getting late.
Forget the car
and forget your date.

When I was young
we were in by seven.
Now you expect
to stay 'til eleven?

Get off the phone
we need to talk.
When I was young
we had to walk.

Read a book.
Study your lessons.
Learn to cook
and count your blessin's.

Mind your manners,
don't chew gum.
What do you want?
You look like a bum.

You're lazy, incompetent,
useless, and crazy.
If you ever did anything,
it'd amaze me.

We both love you,
we really do.
But you need to respect
an elder or two.

You never listen
to a thing I say
you go ahead
and do it anyway.

—Michael D. Gose

Great literature it is not. But we are not only objects of culture, we are creators of culture, and realizing that helps us realize our own creative juices. No matter how limited our talent, the creative process affirms our humanity as well as the occasional joy in our lives.

Field Trips

It is definitely simpler to teach students in your own classroom than it is to take them on a field trip. Any field trip is fraught with potential problems. As a high school teacher I remember a year when all remaining field trips were cancelled after one particular day in which there had been three separate field trips. On one of the three field trips a student had gotten into a fistfight with the bus driver. On another, four students had vanished. And on the third a student had managed to climb into the alligator pen at the zoo.

Nonetheless I've always been a sucker for field trips and if the school couldn't afford buses, I'd take walking field trips, or trips on public transportation. It was probably on field trips that I developed the habit of counting everyone in a group every few minutes.

It takes a minimum of two adults for a field trip, one to lead the students and one to follow them. Keeping an eye out for restrooms is a primary preoccupation. Noticing reasonable places for students to buy something to eat is fairly necessary. The leader has to watch out for lost belongings, make sure there are no fistfights, watch traffic, establish checkpoints, time limits, and a departure point. The teacher encourages good manners and gives directions.

But it is what you don't know that you just can't plan for. I determined to take my fourth-grade class to a historical part of the city, and to use public transportation to get there. We had bus passes, but the initial concern was that the first bus that came may not have room for the full class. On this particular day the bus was virtually empty. The bus driver was friendly and it was a brand-new bus. Life was good. For several stops life was good.

Then we came to a series of stops at the public hospital. The people who started getting on the bus looked like they were cast members from a Fellini movie. One of my greatest themes as a teacher is "appreciate differences," and as a reasonably mature adult I'm good with that. But seeing the cast of characters who got onto the bus and stood holding handgrips while hovering over nine-year-olds was disconcerting. My wife, who was once again helping me with a field trip, looked at me from the corner of her eye. We could only imagine what the scene looked like through the eyes of our nine-year-olds.

The first stop, it became apparent, must have been the closest bus stop bench for outpatients from the burn clinic. The second stop must have been the bench closest to the mental health clinic. I guarantee that no matter how compassionate a person you are, you would not want to see any one of those persons in an alley at night. The burn patients—and your heart would go out to each of them—looked like mummies, all wrapped in gauze. Men and women, many of whom must have been in great pain, peered out of peep holes at our healthy set of fourth-graders. In fact my kids were great. They barely stared, but suddenly the noise level on the bus dropped precipitously.

But if the burn victims were startling, it was difficult to believe that the next few who boarded the bus were outpatients instead of escapees from a prison for the criminally insane. One young man in a trench coat, with greasy, longish dark hair, twitched and kept looking furtively over his shoulder—and he had drool on his chin. A middle-aged woman with unnaturally reddish-blond hair, a lime-green alpaca coat, and a lavender blouse, was apparently talking to someone, but certainly not to anyone on the bus. Most of this small group who got onto the bus had bus passes. I could not imagine that any of them could actually make change.

The burn victims may have looked scary, but it didn't stop them from recognizing what was truly scary. They moved very quickly to the back of the bus. The mentally challenged filled up the front. Standing, they towered over my nine-year-olds, who sat, self-contained, peeking left and right, and apparently feeling more secure than they probably should have felt. Not one of them freaked out. But I am rather certain all pupils' pupils were extremely dilated.

In teaching, like life, you set out in any number of directions, and as Jim Herndon says, it's the accidental joys that are the true rewards along those paths.

A Caper

This is the first public establishment of guilt on this matter: the parties involved until the time of this reading still blame each other.

For two years, our Foreign Language Department chairperson and French teacher feuded about desks. It seems one year the school bought them both some new desks, some large, some small. The desks were divided about evenly the first year and then the second year the department chairperson went for uniformity and transferred enough large desks from the French teacher's room to make a full classroom of the large desks in his classroom, which meant the French teacher had all the small desks in her room. One year and six months later (and after a long series of confrontations and memos to the principal) the diminutive French teacher took her fair share of the large desks back in a lunch-period raid (it was not unlike Liechtenstein invading Germany).

After school that very same day the department chairperson, predictably, reconfiscated the "stolen" desks and returned them to their "rightful" place. Thus issued another series of threats, confrontations, and memos. Then late one Sunday night, anonymous phantoms struck with a nighttime musical chairs ploy. Imagine the two teachers' surprise Monday morning when they opened their respective classrooms to find their usual desks missing, and having been replaced with previously discarded desks—desks with broken seats, rust, and the inevitable wood carving featuring the "F words." How totally "abominable." They both went immediately to the principal, sitting uncomfortably side by side on the bench outside of his office, refusing to speak to anyone until the principal arrived. When each realized that both classrooms had been "vandalized," each came to the separate conclusion that the other had changed the desks in both classrooms to divert suspicion. Of course neither thought the situation was funny. And to my knowledge, they both still think the other perpetrated this foul hoax, even though coach and P.E. teacher Buck Horton has been blamed for it for all these years. In actuality, Laurenzo Giotto did it. Ha!

Philip

Perhaps my best story to suggest the joys and the challenges of teaching, as well as the principles of gamesmanship, is about one of those field trips that I have admitted I enjoy.

I have known at least since I was in seventh grade that good acting goes with good gamesmanship. An eighth-grader on the school's basketball team when I was in junior high school had a well-earned reputation of getting referees to make calls in his favor, not so much because he had been fouled but because he made it look like he had been fouled. That was one of the many lessons I learned in school that had nothing to do with the official curriculum.

Years later I was leading an extended field trip. We stopped at an exquisite little town for lunch. We were afraid, rightly so, that the students would not be back on time so that we could stay on schedule. We made a huge deal about everyone being back on time. Heeding my admonition, all but one of the students were, indeed, back in time. And then we waited and waited. We waited for forty minutes. We sent people out looking for this person, who was named Philip. (That is his name—why protect the guilty?) It was to no avail.

If you do finally find the person you've been waiting for and he is still alive, what do you do? Of course you feel like you'd like to kill him, but that's not a viable option. Maybe you'd like to leave him, but you are far from home and that's not a good option either. Needless to say the other teacher and all the other students were more than miffed. They were the ones who cooperated only to spend forty minutes sitting in the hot, stuffy bus. Something rather dramatic needed to happen to the student, if only to appease the angry mob. Even Philip's friends were disassociating themselves from Philip. No one thought any harm had actually come to Philip. Philip was just like that.

Despite being a bit eccentric and bugging everyone to distraction, everyone knew Philip was really a sweetheart. He was a loveable guy, who'd never deliberately would hurt anyone. He was a champ of a guy. So it was ordinarily reasonably possible to tolerate him for being so spacey, so flaky, so otherworldly. Despite his flights of fantasy no one ever really got mad at Philip, at least for very long.

Nonetheless, there had to be obvious consequences or the remainder of the long field trip would fall apart. As a teacher what do you do? Breaking his thumbs was probably against the law, even if he did deserve it. You know, truly, that nothing you do is likely to faze him. Then when he does show up—and eventually it was inevitable that he would—you can't resist wanting to know where he was, even though a principle of good discipline is to deal with the behavior, not the why. And since he was my student, I had to do something. But what?

Philip was a special person. He was frustrating, but special. As angry as I was about him being so late, I knew that this was seen by everyone on the bus as an act of insubordination on his part. And, as I said, I was terribly curious about where he'd been.

My cardinal rule on discipline is to divide and conquer. You should also realize the great importance I consider the peer group has, and Philip's peers were extremely mad about how long they had been sitting in the bus. Something dramatic needed to happen, but truthfully, I knew yelling at Philip would be to no avail. And as I've said, I had to ask him why he was late, even though I know that the answers to that question were fraught with danger.

When Philip finally showed up, I first divided in order to conquer. By the tone of my voice everyone knew, or thought they knew, that I meant business. With my sternest demeanor I ordered Philip to come with me across the street. The students all lined up eagerly along the windows on that side of the bus to watch, but, importantly, none of them could hear us.

Dramatically, playing to my audience, I poked my finger toward Philip's chest. But to Philip, I asked curiously, "Where were you?"

"I was watching the ducks."

Of course! While our "normal" students were finding a McDonald's and shopping, Philip had found a small creek with ducks. Naturally he was fascinated. And he had (and has) a much sharper sense of wonder than of time. What else would Philip have been doing but watching the ducks? How mad can you get at a kid who loses his sense of time watching ducks?

I went ahead and talked with him calmly about how his friends were probably going to tear him from limb to limb. But that's not what I want to impress upon you the reader. During this calm conversation I was gesticulating wildly. I would throw my hands up in the air. Mostly I'd use my index finger to point excitedly at his chest in short thrusts. All the students on the bus were delighted to see Philip get reamed, and no one seemed to notice they didn't actually hear shouting. Therefore their anger was mollified. Philip was obviously really getting it.

After a while I stopped and strode to the bus, Philip in tow. You would have thought I had him by the ear. I sat in the front in an "obvious" huff. I did overhear a student ask Philip what Gose had to say. Philip answered, "Not much." No one believed him. When we made our next stop I assigned two willing students to be Philip's bodyguards.

Should Philip have been on time? Yes. Did he need to learn to take more responsibility? Yes. Was I irritated that he was late? Definitely. Did

I believe he was watching the ducks? Most definitely. Do I like how I handled this? Absolutely. It was hilarious. I did discipline Philip. But I also protected him. I didn't take it personally. I enjoyed my role, my performance, my gamesmanship. The group moved on from the incident, feeling, more or less falsely, that there was still some order in the universe. Among those of us who still know and love Philip, the story has become legend.

TEACHING FOUR-YEAR-OLDS

The chutzpah it takes to write an account about what it means to be a teacher comes from my initial interest in trying to figure out how to be an effective teacher. From my very first teaching job I had the idea that I needed to teach people of all ages to better understand what it truly means to teach any particular age group. While I've spent my professional time teaching college, high school, and elementary school, I looked for an opportunity to teach preschool children.

The opportunity came when my wife and I offered to teach a class for four-year-olds at our church. The fact that my own four-year-old daughter was in that class was an extra incentive, but I had been looking to teach that age group. I will admit that I did it with as much dread and fear of failure as I've felt toward anything I have ever done. I knew my classical education was not going to be terribly helpful for teaching a preliterate group.

Because I had already taught high school and elementary school, and having developed a special fondness for curriculum development, I spent several hours planning all that we would do for the "semester." It was only a one-hour class, once a week. But my wife and I wanted to be well prepared. We wanted to include a story or two, art, some songs, some talk, and some use of media. We wanted to do lots of stuff. And it was only eighteen weeks—a piece of cake.

And we needed all of the material we had developed for the eighteen weeks the very first night. We needed all of it. And if we hadn't had plenty of snacks, we would have come up short.

We had a slumber party for the girls. Why we were determined to do that for four-year-old girls, I'm not sure, but we did. I learned a lot during that class, and I gathered some lifelong memories.

The girls showed up at our house with their Hello Kitty, Barbie Doll, or Scooby Do sleeping bags. They fought, argued, bickered, complained, pushed, shoved, provoked, disagreed, insisted, and took exception—late into the night and early into the morning. I never remembered having had such a strong feeling of having made such a mistake in judgment as I did in having gone along with the idea of having this party. The girls were relentless. We could hardly wait for the mothers (and it was only mothers, no fathers) to pick their "cherubs" up. I was counting the minutes.

But what was so amazing, and revealing, was that as they were leaving the girls, without exception, asked—no, demanded—that they have another slumber party the next week. Assuredly we did not, for our own sanity. But the girls' insistence was a revelation. We were focused on the hassles, but the four-year-olds were immediately and intensely involved in the activity, in the working out of their own lives. They were, to use a modern metaphor, in the middle of a live-action computer game. They were having a ball. We, the authority figures, were on the verge of nervous breakdowns, but the kids were having a great time. They were thoroughly involved, looking out for their own interests.

All the rest of a life span became clearer to me: We are born into our sandbox, have a great time messing it up, and then return to our maker. We create most of our own hassles because, apparently, we enjoy them, no matter how unpleasant they superficially seem to others.

The other memories of our class are more out of context. One boy amused us greatly, although we made a vow never to let him date our daughter, by drawing penises on everything. He drew penises on Noah's ark, on trees, on all the people, even on a rock. We tried not to think about Freud.

Every four-year-old is "attention deficit," but we were particularly distracted by the young boy with Velcro-fastening shoes who would open and close the Velcro constantly for very long periods of time. And the son of a psychiatrist and psychologist once called after one of the girls, "Come back, we can work this out." But my favorite recollection was of my role in supervising the boys in the bathroom. I supervised, to make sure everything went okay, and to make sure no full rolls of toilet paper were dumped into the toilet bowl.

One young boy, who was to grow up to be nearly 6'6", was not, in fact, at that time tall enough to stand and pee into the bowl. I was momentarily alarmed to think he might pee all over the floor. It was not a problem. He moved up immediately to the front of the toilet, pulled out his penis, and nonplused by the height of the toilet, stretched his penis like a rubber snake, up, up, up, and over the toilet rim. He relieved himself easily and without mistake. That I held my laughter is great testimony to my sensibilities as a teacher!

Ah, the unexpected joy along the way.

BONUS SECTION: REVENGE

I've added this bonus section because the following stories are not representative of what usually happens with teachers. Although these particular stories of mine are not typical of what teachers actually do, I suspect that they are fairly consistent with what many teachers might like to do if they were presented with similar opportunities. I am reminded of the teacher Mr. Hand in the movie *Fast Times at Ridgemont High*. Mr. Hand told students not to waste "his" classroom time; he compared it to them not wanting him to waste their private time. Mr. Hand wreaked a certain revenge by showing up at a student's home to reiterate that message.

For my part, I have had the great good fortune to have been a resident faculty member in my university's European program. My family and I had the good fortune to live under the same roof with approximately fifty mostly nineteen-year-olds, once in Heidelberg, Germany, and twice in London. Any non-teacher seems to automatically think that teaching, and having room and board covered, while living in Europe is equivalent to being on vacation. Most any teacher would certainly grab such an opportunity, recognizing it as one of the only ways a teacher can afford to spend substantial time abroad, but would also know what a daunting undertaking it would be to teach *and* live with students.

Most teachers are such nice people that they wouldn't have done some of the things that I've done in a residential setting. But they're not so nice that they're not likely to appreciate my dastardly deeds. On behalf of teachers everywhere I invoked an eye for an eye, a bone for a bone. I am unapologetic. I didn't harm anyone physically. In fact I will argue that my acts of retribution had the prospects of being great lessons in life. But the joy of inflicting my responses to student behavior is what I would emphasize here. I struck blows for all teachers everywhere.

Some of my acts were first-degree acts, carefully planned, while others were more on the scale of voluntary manslaughter.

We participated in the Heidelberg program relatively early in my career. I had the very brightest of my college's sophomores. They would literally go on to win all the major and minor academic awards in their graduating class. But as sophomores they were, well, still rather sophomoric. I had students who probably hadn't had a B since seventh-grade P.E. class. Some of these august students were, nonetheless, still humble about their lives as scholars. But some weren't.

A couple of particular students still confused themselves with the cat's meow. That's okay with me as long as the performance is there. But I've also found some truth to the saying that students need to raise their level of accomplishment to succeed at the next level.

I suppose it's also important to add that I invariably have a policy that a student can drop one test. Otherwise this would be a story about being vindictive instead of being just.

Anyway, some of this otherwise accomplished group took a look at their essay question—and then ignored it. Since much of my academic success has been due to the influence of my own high school teacher, Mr. John Daly (who drilled into us "R.T.P."—"read the problem"), I have a particular sense of how important it is to actually answer the question of an essay exam. It's not an entirely novel idea, and it's an important one. Daly's assumption, and my own, is that any essay that does not answer the question is a failure. A few students who had almost never had Bs on an assignment received the grades they had earned: Fs.

It takes either guts or stupidity to give Fs to students you live with. Since they could drop an exam anyway, I was in good humor about the results. However, two students in particular were indignant, most indignant. They demanded high grades because (a) they liked what they had done; (b) I should like what they had done; (c) it must not have been a good question; (d) why wouldn't they get partial credit; (e) life's not fair; or (f) some or all of the above.

With unusual graciousness (for me) I explained the demands of the essay, the advantages of answering the question, and the survival of the fittest. And, yes, reluctantly, I reminded them that they would be able to drop this exam, but, what, really, was the point if they didn't raise their level of accomplishment? (You can assume this role if you are right, if you've provided a safety net, if you really do have your students' long-term best interests at heart, and if you are committed to the same high standards for yourself.)

For me it was critical that we did live in the same house together. It was easier to hold each other fully responsible. Every teacher has had the insufferably excellent student who scoffs at the teacher with a humorless grin. In this situation I was able to do the grinning. And it felt great. It also felt great, if in a different kind of way, when these same two students wrote superior essays the next time around.

Of course there are many other such stories that I can tell (and activities I was able to undertake) because I lived in the same house. There was the daughter of the general who wouldn't keep her room clean. At room-check time I got a pitchfork and photographer and went to her room for pictures to send to her father. Of course that did not mean that her room was ever actually cleaned, but a good time was had by all. Teachers so often feel victimized by students; these residential situations let me also be a protagonist and antagonist in response to student behavior. It gave me a real sense of (temporary) freedom.

Then there was the student who wouldn't pick up his own dishes in the common areas. One evening I gathered all the dirty dishes and placed them in his bed. (By the way, his name is Philip Suggs, and while other names in this book should be changed to protect the innocent, this story is about Philip Suggs.) Coming in late that night Philip actually slept in bed with the dirty dishes. The next morning he expressed some surprise that the dishes were in his bed and claimed he had no idea why anyone would pick that particular surprise for him. Go figure. Once again though, I felt I was striking a blow for all teachers for all time.

Within a house setting it was not even necessary to be fair in extracting justice. I picked on one particular student only because it was so irritating that she was one of the world's nicest people. She was the least likely person to get into trouble, innocent in the very best sense of that word. Our men's and women's floors were separate, and there were certainly rules about what was appropriate behavior for the respected sexes on these floors. There was also some expectation that the rooms stay clean enough to protect against health hazards. Ordinarily a resident advisor did room checks, but if things got bad enough, the resident faculty member was expected to conduct the check.

Well, things *had* apparently gotten bad enough that I was expected to do the room check. Rather than making it odious, I took my video camera and a small group of investigators from room to room. I was like the pied piper, picking up a crowd as I went. I reserved the best surprise for the student I've accused of being so nice. The sexiest guy and Maria's roommates were in on it. Of course this was the neatest, cleanest, most pristine room of all. Surely the room would pass inspection and we could move on. But, what, wait, we did not check under her bed. Give me the stick—let's check under the bed. What, hmm, there's something under here, wait a minute, there I've got it, my God, what is this? Oh, my! Is this what I think it is? Here, I'll hold it up for the camera. A pair of men's red boxer shorts.

Maria turned redder than the boxer shorts. And for seconds it was incredulous to her that they could be there under her bed. For moments she was still unsuspecting, trying to think how they could be there. Then this unsuspecting person knew she had been had, by me, by her roommates, by John who provided the boxers. But still she blushed. She's now a lawyer in Boston, although there's not necessarily a cause-and-effect relationship here.

Of course I'm way too proud of such stories of revenge. Besides my own immaturity and perverseness, I do think that this pride is an indication of the pent-up feelings a teacher ordinarily never gets to express because of the limitations of the classroom. But I suspect the hidden feelings are, nonetheless, there for many if not most of us.

My very favorite story in these regards is also, I think, the most germane to teaching. I work very hard to inculcate a reputation of being demanding, and of not letting anything slide. Certainly I want to be seen as firm and fair, and as having great humor when everyone is being responsible. So, what was I to do when, first semester, one of our legends, who was taking my class as an elective, credit/no credit, skipped my final exam? Obviously no one before or after had skipped one of my final exams. It was inconceivable. Yet it was also true that this endearing student could flunk the final and still have more than enough points to pass the class. Nonetheless, all students were supposed to take the final. And, worse yet, all the class members knew that this student had not asked permission to miss the final, and had, in fact, made a special point to have arrived in Munich early enough so that he could be drinking beer at the Hofbräuhaus while the other students were taking their exam.

What was a teacher to do? Flunk him? Not likely. Let it go? Also not likely. I did announce to the class, and later to the entire house, that there would be consequences, that they would be appropriate, and that everyone would know, beyond a shadow of a doubt that the consequences would more than match Blaine's dastardly deed.

Of course at the time I was still dumbfounded as to what to do. Fortunately I had most of the same students the second semester. An idea occurred to me and a plan evolved. Over the next weeks students would remark that they had not yet seen any consequences. I like to use the biblical quote, "Vengeance is mine, thus saith the Lord." Using that quote had sacrilegious implications, but I felt I was justified in being a bit over the top in my remarks.

Among the many things that Blaine was known for was his fanaticism about taking pictures and his obsession with the cult movie *The Rocky Horror Picture Show*. Blaine even brought his Rocky Horror costume with him to Germany. He was able to wear it at our Halloween party and at midnight showings of the *Rocky Horror Picture Show*, which even played periodically in Heidelberg. And as the resident faculty member, I had access to a key to Blaine's room.

I had to wait until final exam time second semester for my revenge. Except for field trips when we were all away, it was the only time all the students were out of the house. I had waited all semester long and the adrenaline was coursing through my veins as I used my own key to get into our main office and borrow the key to Blaine's room. Maybe cat burglars break in for the adrenaline rush more than for what they take. Certainly I was very excited. And I was in good luck. I was concerned that I'd have to load Blaine's very expensive camera to get my revenge, but fortune — maybe it was destiny or providence — held and there were plenty of shots left on the roll in his camera. (My wife, a reluctant co-conspirator, agreed to be my cameraperson — I dared not use a student's help because there were no kept secrets in the house.)

I was able to find Blaine's makeup and the Rocky Horror costume quickly. I put on the white facial cream, the black lipstick, the hair grease, the macabre black-and-white costume. I had also brought with me large signs that read, "Blaine in bed," "Blaine in the shower," "Blaine at his desk," and "Blaine in the window," except of course, when we took the photos it was me in Blaine's room, in Blaine's makeup, in Blaine's costume. I was using Blaine's camera and Blaine's film to take pictures of *moi*, signs in hand, exacting my revenge.

Then I put everything back as I had found it. I hoped I'd made no conspicuous mistake. At dinner I announced that I had now taken my revenge. I would not say what it was, but surely, I announced, they all would eventually find out what it had been and recognize for now and ever more not to mess with the teacher.

I could so readily imagine the moment that was so sure to come, and did come: the moment when Blaine developed his film and found to his own rocky horror the pictures from his camera, that he had paid to develop, that were of me in his room, in his makeup and in his clothes. The moment when he knew beyond the shadow of a doubt that I had enjoyed myself in his room more than he had enjoyed himself at the Hofbräuhaus. That story would spread, not from my lips, but from student to student, almost as fast as the speed of light, no matter where they were on the globe. All of us would know and agree that once again there was order in the world.

I am a teacher!

SUMMARY FOR PART ONE

I have taken many cuts at my drafts for this book. I remain most surprised that I've not once included a chapter on discipline. Certainly maintaining classroom discipline is the most fundamental issue in teaching; it's more basic by far than the official curriculum. Having to maintain discipline among a large group of non-adults who do not necessarily have much in common with us is a feat. But eventually discipline is just another job condition. It comes with the territory. The meaning of teaching comes with the actual personal relationships that lead to the need for a disciplinary action.

So, what are the consequences of being a teacher? We become part of the special rhythms of a school year. I doubt that any profession other than farmer involves such definite routines and rhythms that repeat on a yearly basis.

Most teachers start having anxiety dreams and restless sleep in late August as we anticipate the beginning of another school year. September and the start of the school year is like spring training in baseball: it's full of hope and expectation, with each teacher thinking this year they will go to the World Series. It's generally a pattern of falling energy levels to Thanksgiving, with a lull between Thanksgiving and Christmas. Some amount of restoring energy occurs over the winter break, which is usually two weeks. A new, if lower, high in January slopes downwards toward June 1, and then drops precipitously after June 1. Then comes the very necessary summer respite.

Teachers thrive on the pronounced starts and finishes. Very few professions have such punctuation along the way. Within this routine, as we teach the curriculum to our students and weave in encounters with administrators and parents along the way, we are affected. Most teachers laugh a great deal each day, even if they have to stifle it until later so as not to embarrass a student, or to keep students from thinking their miscreant misbehavior is somehow okay.

The cumulative effect of teaching is fairly subtle and occurs over a long period of time. These effects are, certainly, moderated by the particular personality of the individual teacher. In a way each of us is like a stalagmite, with the existential meaning of teaching built up in the small moments along the time span of a career. From the first deposited memory one is a stalagmite, but the stalagmite becomes much more impressive as more mineral deposits are made over an increasing span of years. Nonetheless, the net effects then do include that we seem, despite the wear and tear, to stay younger than those in our same age groups. Students who are experiencing culture as novices keep us apprised of changes in heroes, music, computers, sports, TV, and movies.

We are forced, even coerced, to be less selfish. Despite our limited income and the demands on our time, we continually find ourselves going the extra mile, and, true to Aristotle's idea about habits of virtue, we find ourselves becoming more virtuous.

Inevitably we must learn to appreciate diversity because of the care we offer to each student who becomes our charge. With Dostoevsky, we find that we do learn through suffering (whether we like it or not).

Some of the influences of teaching are somewhat paradoxical. Because we are overstimulated by so many people in a small space, we become irritable, but at the same time we are in fact often more patient—while we're irritable about the little stuff, we're patient with the larger picture.

We also tend to become both more pessimistic and more optimistic: pessimistic about large-scale changes, optimistic about the changes an individual student can make.

And, please read this carefully because the metaphor I am about to use might otherwise seem negative. In Franz Kafka's story *The Metamorphosis*, the narrator turns into a cockroach. It's not entirely an unfitting image of what we necessarily become as teachers. In the documentary *The Hellstrom Chronicle*, the case is made that insects have the best longtime prospects of survival on the planet. They have evolved with the greatest immunity to all perils.

Teachers are a bit like that. If you are not a teacher you have absolutely no idea of how many educational fads outsiders have tried to inflict upon us; how many new laws have been passed on what we must be responsible for; how we have accommodated major changes in immigration, special education, students from single-parent families, mandates, commissions, changes in administration and school boards; of changes in standardized tests that no longer reflect what we are teaching in our particular schools; or our roles as kicking posts for political opportunists.

No wonder there is so much agitation. Education is the last ultimate political act. Naturally everyone wants to tell teachers what to do. We sort through the static. On very rare occasions we actually hear a better idea and modify our practice.

Then we close our classroom doors, look our students in the eyes, and continue to go about our business. Each year we develop a tougher shell, but somehow each year we also become a slightly better person.

This is our experience as teachers.

Part 2

Essence, n. 1. The permanent as contrasted with the accidental element of being. 2. The individual, real, or ultimate nature of a thing especially as opposed to its existence. 3. That which makes something what it is; the fundamental nature (of something). 4. In philosophy, true substance. (*Webster's New Collegiate Dictionary* and *Webster's New World Dictionary*)

The Essence of What It Means to Be a Teacher

While we teach, we learn.

—Seneca

(Franz Kafka's) interest in me was a wonderful gift to me. I was always conscious of this. Once I even expressed myself in this sense to him. "Do I not waste your time? I am so stupid. You give me so much and I give you nothing." Kafka was plainly embarrassed by my words. . . . "You are not stupid. So stop using such phrases, by which you will only force me to admit that I enjoy your youthful devotion and understanding."

—Janovich Gustav

[What must we do as teachers?] Face our classes with all the courage and hope we can muster . . . probe the mystery of what happens when teachers and students meet . . . sort out our own thoughts . . . not expect easy answers . . . nor be unnerved should we encounter pockets of fog.

—Philip Jackson

TEACHERS AS ART

Before discussing the essence of what it means to be a teacher, I would like to briefly suggest that teachers, in a sense, are *art*. I am not talking about the science and art of teaching here. I am suggesting the sense in which teachers are the artistic outcomes of so many other people's creative efforts. I don't want to take this analogy too far. I believe that teachers are independent agents who exercise free will. But any success we have as teachers is usually a result of the many positive influences we have had, whether of former teachers, friends, family members, colleagues, or students. I would not be the same teacher except for my fifth-grade teacher, Miss Hartman; my English teacher, Mrs. Coleman; my history teacher, Mr. Daly; my college teacher, Dr. Lewis Owen; a university professor, Elliot Eisner; my own students like Jeanne Spitler, Frank Cruz, Charlie Park, Tanja Carter, Chris Grimm, and Lisa Kodama; administrators like Ray Cook, Howard White, and John Wilson; colleagues like Larry Giacomino, Paul Begin, JoAnn Taylor, Art Walsh, and Bob King; friends like Raquel Alvarez, John Ellis, and Tami Snow; staff like Dorothy Bettencourt, Allen Haren, and Bob Escudero; authors like James Herndon and Jenny Gray; parents of students like the Pauls; or my wife, Janice, and daughter, Creedance, and son-in-law, Chris (who say to me, "You are such a teacher").

Teachers are open to a wider spectrum of creative forces than any group that I can think of. Sometimes it is almost overwhelming. Sometimes the stimulation is too much. Most of us cannot imagine a longer school year than the typical 180 days. But my point here is to argue, if only in a limited sense, that while we do see ourselves as independent free agents, practicing our profession behind the closed doors of the classroom, we must also recognize with both pride and humility that we are the products of the fruitful and artistic labor of so many who care for us.

When someone says about us that we are so old we belong in a museum, it might be agreed that we deserve the honor: we are among society's most classic productions!

KNOWLEDGE AND VIRTUE

Philip Jackson, a hero of mine since I first read his book *Life in Classrooms*, doubts the efficacy of figuring out what it means to be a teacher. Jackson (1986, p. 89) "denies the possibility of our ever arriving upon an enduring definition of what it means to be a teacher." He also says, "most teachers I have known seldom wonder aloud about the meaning of teaching," adding that teachers are "too busy doing what they have to do."

I certainly understand and appreciate his points. Nonetheless, for the bulk of this book I have argued that teachers implicitly do know what it means to be a teacher, especially "existentially," in terms of their own experiences as teachers. Unlike when I was teaching in elementary or high school, I have more recently had the time that a college professor has to think and write about the "true meaning of being a teacher." But I would emphasize that in doing this reflective work, I feel like I still have the heart of a tenth-grade English teacher. While I do not really quarrel with Philip Jackson's points, I do believe that I have created in this work a significant expression of what it does mean to be a teacher, existentially.

In fact my own effort, while different in character, is similar to that Jackson describes in his *Practice of Teaching*. Jackson (1986, p. 95) says that his book "is an attempt to locate teaching within what Toulmin calls 'a network of relations.' Its [teaching's] place within that network that is its *ultimate* [emphasis added] source of meaning and significance." For my own part, I've used the twelve themes of my first section of this book to locate teaching in such a network of relations. But philosophically I quarrel with Jackson's use of the world "ultimate." "Ultimate" is a word associated with "essence" rather than "existence," and it thus suggests a meaning beyond any network of relations. While by definition we have at best an incomplete knowledge of what is *essential*, I believe that it is still imperative to distill out the essence of teaching from its existential conditions. Such attempts to realize the fundamental, ultimate reality of teaching are undertaken far too seldom.

So, what's the essence of what it means to be a teacher? Amos Alcott (*The Teacher*) believed that there are essential truths and that that has implications for teaching. Alcott says: "The true teacher defends his pupils against his own personal influence. He inspires self-distrust. He guides their eyes from himself to the spirit that quickens him. He will have no disciple." This point of view about being a guide has much in common with Socrates' idea of the teacher as an intellectual midwife, while having greater religious overtones with this idea of "the spirit." Certainly the metaphor of guide or midwife is critical to understanding what it means to be a teacher. Through the folly of the first year of teaching; despite the limitations of the job conditions and our failures; regardless of the degree of success, with the joys that come and in the face of honor and betrayal; against administrators' abuses of power; working through the dilemmas that confront us; and having courage in spite of our vulnerability, we teach the curriculum accepting our roles as guides and even as "intellectual midwives." Intellectual instruction is of paramount importance and this is readily acknowledged in school. But there is more to it than just that.

If there are Platonic implications in Alcott's ideas about being an instructional guide, there are Aristotelian implications about virtue evident in Jonathan Kozol's ideas. Kozol recognizes the importance of the tangible example of the teacher and stresses the importance of modeling "virtue." In *On Being a Teacher* (1981, p. 20), Kozol says: "The hidden curriculum . . . is the teacher's own integrity and lived conviction. The most memorable lesson is not what is written to the student on a sheet of yellow lined paper in the lesson pad; nor is it the clumsy sentence published (and "illustrated") in the standard and official text. It is the message which is written in the teacher's eyes throughout the course of his or her career. It is the lesson which endures a lifetime."

Kozol is not failing to appreciate the teaching of the official curriculum so much as emphasizing a more inclusive understanding of teaching. This understanding includes an emphasis on virtue as well as knowledge. Aristotle says, "virtue, then, is of two kinds, intellectual and moral. Intellectual virtue owes its inception and its growth chiefly to *instruction*, and for this very reason needs time and experience. Moral goodness, on the other hand, is the result of habit." Thus Aristotle emphasizes intellectual instruction *and* habits of virtue. Besides instruction, Aristotle places an emphasis on both virtue and examples of virtue. In this regard, Kozol emphasizes the importance of the lived example of the teacher as a way of inculcating such virtue.

For me, Rabbi Zev Schostak has best captured the essence of what it means to be both a teacher of the mind (knowledge) and of the heart (virtue).

In the World of Tomorrow

I am the most fortunate one for I am eternal
Others live merely in the world of today; I live in the world of tomorrow.
Others find purpose in the transient and the temporal;
I find meaning in the enduring and the eternal
For I am charged with that most sacred mission—
To transmit all that our forebears lived for, loved for, and died for to the
    next generation

I span the generations—making the wisdom of the past live now so that
  the future will have meaning
I make wisdom live, for I am no mere bearer of knowledge

I do not simply teach the mind
I reach the heart and—when
I reach the heart
I touch the soul

To those who say two generations hence what will I be if not a distant
  memory, I respond:
Though the mind fades,
memories linger
Though the body fails,
the spirit prevails
Though the scroll burns,
the letters dance in the air.
Though I cease to be, through my children I live eternally.

Truly this is my destiny for I live in the world to tomorrow—
I am a teacher!

—Rabbi Zev Schostak

I could almost end the book with that poem.

FULL CIRCLE

I certainly appreciate what both Alcott and Kozol have to say about teaching the intellectual and the moral as critical to a full understanding of the meaning of teaching. I am deeply moved by Schostak's poem. In all their responses to the question of what it means to be a teacher, their emphasis is understandably on the teacher. But it also seems important here, in conclusion, to emphasize the potential the students have as our teachers as well. Tolstoy celebrated his own experience of two of his own students, one of whom he describes as "a peasant boy, with the bare knowledge of reading." He says: "It seemed so strange and offensive to me that I, the author of 'Childhood,' who had had the certain success and had earned recognition for artistic talent from a cultivated Russian public,—that I, in the matter of art, not only should be unable to teach anything to an eleven-year-old Semka or Fedka or to help them, but I only with difficulty and in a happy moment of excitement should be able to follow and understand them."

Certainly students, often at the most unexpected times, guide us to the "spirit" and model for us "integrity and lived conviction." The teacher role is never truly independent from relationships with students. Indeed our lives as teachers are defined within and by our "network of such relations." These networks dominate our existence as teachers, and while we ordinarily avoid too much rhetoric about the *essence* of teaching—because ours is not a pretentious occupation, and because we are too often humbled not only by our failures but by the kindness and thanks that punctuate our careers—we are concerned about the fundamentals of our existence.

Our understanding of what it means to be a teacher may be incomplete, it may be mysterious. Certainly it includes a realization that we are guides to knowledge and examples of our own lived convictions. But an even deeper appreciation of what it means to be a teacher comes when our efforts have come full circle and it is the student who has blessed us as a guide, as an example, as someone who affirms us. Thus I close with another poem, a poem given to me by a student. It is a far richer treasure than I've ever deserved, one that keeps me ever mindful of what it, ideally, means to be a teacher. It was a "gift" to me and I share it as a gift from me to all teachers.

Gift

A whisper of a thought
has crossed my mind.
Only a whisper,
As the full realization
Has not come . . .
But soon it will be time.
Goodbye
(Remember)

I've sat in the corner
All year long.
Watching you,
And when you watched back:
When I wasn't looking.

Playing our game.
Together—Alone, of
People.
(Listen)

You have listened,
With ears of Golden Honey.
Melting only to speak
of education.
Reading my world
Which I have set on paper, to
Understand.
(Know)

You to me are different:
Because of everyone that knows you,
They all have a different "you"
To them.
You are not Mike,
You are not Mr.
You are truly
"Teacher . . ."
(Live)

—Beth Wine

For the truest meaning of teaching is found in some measure, whether we are atheists, agnostics, or believers, in those blessed moments when we, with our variety of understandings, stand outside ourselves, transcend ourselves, are both teacher and student, and realize our connection with and commitment to participation in, oneness with the universe, our solidarity with all the others, the spirit, God.

We. Teachers. Live.

Appendix A

Recommendations to Improve Teaching

- Buckets and buckets of paint
- No more than one faculty meeting per semester
- Ban tests on Fridays
- Instead of criticizing functioning adults for reading at the eighth-grade level, recognize the eighth-graders for matching an adult reading level
- Quit using "grade levels" to report test results; by definition one-half of the students have to be below grade level
- Hire permanent substitute teachers to give all teachers one free day a month, and trust them to use the day as they need to use it
- Quit making any teacher use IEPs (individualized education programs)
- For the most part, if a teacher doesn't coach the sport, don't have the sport
- Ask the teachers what resources or help they need to do the job they are trying to do instead of giving them yet another in-service that will require them to do more than they already have time to do
- Give more student-friendly standardized tests, and only report the student's best score of basic skill and best evidence of individual accomplishment
- Do not have bulletin announcements over the school public address system

- Have at least one school within a school per high school
- Do not require specialized subject matter classes until the student has demonstrated interest as well as basic skills
- Send a teacher a thank-you note
- Give young and creative teachers the room to grow

Appendix B

Quiz

1. Not including textbooks, who spends the most money for materials in the classroom?
   a. The federal government
   b. The state government
   c. The county government
   d. The city government
   e. The school board
   f. The parents
   g. The students
   h. The teacher
2. On the Scholastic Assessment Tests (SATs), students are, overall, still within about four right answers (raw score) of the all-time American high on SAT scores. Students have been able to do this because of
   a. The abundance of two-parent families having extra time
   b. The emigration of students who were not raised in the language of the SAT tests to other countries
   c. The abundance of new funding for public education
   d. Teachers
3. The general condition of teacher salaries and benefits is best defined by the following statement:
   a. The past thirty years has seen the best overall support of teachers in world history
   b. Teachers are underpaid
   c. Both of the above

4. Excellent teacher are usually rewarded by
   a. Higher class sizes
   b. Higher class sizes
   c. Higher class sizes
   d. Higher class sizes
5. True or True: In the Gallop Poll, teachers rank only behind the clergy and doctors in terms of greatest contributions to society.
6. The average amount of square footage per person in a classroom is about
   a. 25
   b. 50
   c. 75
   d. 100
7. Since the answer to number 6 is A, which is about 5 feet by 5 feet, how could a student or teacher lie down in the space allotted to them?
   a. Be under 5 feet tall
   b. Lie corner to corner
   c. Take someone else's space
   d. Ask for a potty pass and go somewhere else
8. The worst area on any campus is usually
   a. The boys' restroom
   b. The girls' restroom
   c. Wherever it is the kids hide to smoke
   d. The faculty lounge
   e. The science department refrigerator
9. True or False: Those who can do; those who can't do teach; those who can't teach become administrators.
10. The average number of teachers on the various commissions for education change is
    a. 0
11. The greatest controversy on a public school campus is usually
    a. Who parks where?
    b. Who cleans the dirty coffee cups?
    c. How long should the lunch period be?
    d. Should there be a dress code?
    e. The tardiness policy

12. The most pernicious influence on public education is
    a. Television
    b. Rock music
    c. Alcohol
    d. Drugs
    e. Bart Simpson
    f. Candy sales
13. The hero for most teachers is
    a. Socrates
    b. Aristotle
    c. Jaime Escalante
    d. Mel Gibson
14. The most typical car in the teachers' parking lot is
    a. A sports car
    b. A truck
    c. A van
    d. A vehicle that is to cars as Spam is to meat
15. The reasons teachers' mailboxes are in the administrative office is
    a. Because it is convenient to the parking lot
    b. So the principal can check that the teacher is on time
16. Cafeteria lunches remind one of the Woody Allen joke:
    a. Woman A: The lunches taste bad.
    b. Woman B: Yes, and they have such small portions.
17. The day before Christmas vacation is
    a. The best day of the year
    b. The hardest day of the year
    c. Both of the above
18. The recurring nightmare for teachers is
    a. None of the students will sit down or be quiet
    b. They can't find the classroom
    c. They've gone to school and forgotten to get dressed
    d. They will have to go to another after-school meeting
19. True or False: The only thing worse than having a teaching job is not having a teaching job.
20. What goes on in class takes up about 95 percent of a teacher's time and dealing with school administrators about 5 percent. Thus

teachers spend about what percentage of their non-classroom time fretting about administrators?

    a. 100 percent

    b. 99.9 percent

    c. 99.8 percent

    d. 99.75 percent

21. In these times, the last time a classroom was probably cleaned professionally was

    a. Last month

    b. Last year

    c. Sometime in the 1970s

    d. After school yesterday, by the teacher

22. How often is a teacher likely to have enough books for each student?

    a. Never

    b. Anytime, if they want to teach *Silas Marner*

23. Which is true?

    a. Students keep teachers young

    b. Students drive teachers to an early grave

24. Schools would be a lot better without

    a. Back to School nights

    b. School days after June 1

    c. Minimum days

    d. Football coaches

25. The best reason for a school library is:

    a. Books for students to check out

    b. Reference materials for student papers

    c. An extra bathroom

    d. A place to take a class when one has failed to plan a lesson

26. What is most likely to happen in a school restroom?

    a. Going number one

    b. Going number two

    c. Smoking

27. The biggest problem with discipline in school is that schools are

    a. Too soft on students

    b. Too hard on students

28. Should you be able to fire a rifle down a hallway during a classroom period without hitting anyone?

29. The ideal vice principal has much in common with
    a. Attila the Hun
    b. Dick Butkus
    c. The Terminator
    d. Mary Poppins

30. Essay question: Why waste a paid sick day by staying home sick?

31. Unanswerable question: If recalcitrant students sit at the back of the classroom, why do teachers put their desks at the front of the classroom?

32. What color is a blackboard?

33. Chalk dust causes:
    a. Cancer
    b. Allergies
    c. Unsightliness
    d. A mess

34. How many outside interruptions typify a school hour?
    a. 17
    b. 105
    c. 1011
    d. An infinite number

35. Who or what is most likely to interrupt your lesson?
    a. A student with an unrelated question
    b. The school custodian
    c. An announcement on the PA system
    d. A student monitor with a bogus hall pass for a student who needs a smoke

36. A teacher's grade book looks most like
    a. A Kandinsky painting
    b. A Klee painting
    c. A finger painting

37. A teacher can:
    a. Pat and rub his or her head and rub his or her tummy at the same time
    b. Take attendance and teach at the same time

38. Student desks were built for
    a. Comfort
    b. Utility
    c. To punish students for being young
    d. Auto-da-fe (the Inquisition)
39. Which is the bane of starting class?
    a. Prayer
    b. The Pledge of Allegiance
    c. The bulletin
    d. A hangover
40. What annoys teachers most?
    a. Gum
    b. The public combing of hair
    c. Corn nuts
    d. Students who repeatedly say "like" and/or "you know"
41. Teachers would gain more respect if
    a. Administrators treated them with respect
    b. Parents treated them with respect
    c. They received public recognition
    d. They carried a gun
42. Teachers live:
    a. For the teaching moment
    b. From paycheck to paycheck
43. The best way to organize junior high school is
    a. By department
    b. By Zodiac signs
44. Teachers know that the one job they would hate the most is
    a. Superintendent
    b. Principal
    c. Vice principal
    d. School bus driver
45. True or False: Planning a field trip seemed like a good idea at the time.
46. True or False: Shortened minimum day periods are easier to teach.
47. What is most disruptive?
    a. The day of a football game
    b. The day of a school dance

    c. A disaster drill

    d. An in-service training day

48. True or False: Teachers *can* list their addresses and phone numbers in the phone directory because it would never occur to students that their teachers lived in a house.

49. The happiest teachers are those who

    a. Love their subject matter

    b. Teach kids

50. Why do teachers dress like they do?

    a. They are products of the 1960s

    b. They cannot afford to dress better

    c. They know they are treated more like blue-collar workers than professionals

    d. They get up so early they have to dress in the dark

51. The bane of teaching is

    a. Grading papers

    b. Grading papers

    c. Grading papers

    d. Grading papers

52. The best way to get a student's attention is to

    a. Yell

    b. Whisper

    c. Strip naked and run through the aisles hoping someone will notice and pass the word on to other students in the class

53. The best way to handle a recalcitrant student is

    a. Prescription drugs

    b. A referral

    c. A parent conference

    d. A kind word

54. True or False: A community shows its value of education by the condition of the school plant.

55. One-word essay: How does a teacher feel about the fact that the parents who should have come to Back to School Night didn't?

56. The worst supervision duty is

    a. Lunch

    b. Buses

    c. The dance

    d. The football game

    e. The opposite-sex restroom

57. How many encouraging words does a teacher expect to hear from an administrator in a given year?

58. Pretty much we teachers teach to

    a. The top of the class

    b. The middle of the class

    c. The bottom of the class

    d. Whomever we please

59. Students today can be characterized as

    a. Having short attention spans

    b. Having poor grooming habits

    c. Being hyperactive

    d. Being lazy

    e. Acting their age

60. The typical student desk has how many pieces of gum stuck to it?

61. Essay question: Explain why the school air conditioner works in the winter but not in the summer.

References

Aquinas, T. (1948). In A. E. Pegis (Ed.), *The summa theologica*. New York: The Modern Library.

Eisner, E. (1979). *The educational imagination*. New York: MacMillan.

Fader, D. (1976). *The new hooked on books*. New York: Berkley Publishing Corporation.

Gose, M. (1996). Teaching in the 1990s. *Teacher Education Quarterly, 23*(2).

Gray, J. (1969). *The teacher's survival guide*. Belmont: Fearon Teacher Aids.

Herndon, J. (1971). *How to survive in your native land*. New York: Bantam Books.

Herndon, J. (1985). *Notes from a school teacher*. New York: Simon and Schuster.

Jackson, P. (1968). *Life in classrooms*. New York: Holt, Rinehart and Winston, Inc.

Jackson, P. (1986). *The practice of teaching*. New York: Teachers College Press.

Kozol, J. (1981). *On being a teacher*. New York: Continuum.

Zehon, S., and Kolter, J. (1993). *On being a teacher*. Newbury Park: Corwin Press.

About the Author

Michael Gose received his Ph.D. from Stanford University. He has been a fourth-grade teacher, tenth-grade English teacher, director of an experimental school, vice principal, principal, professor, director of secondary education, and chair of the Social Science/Teacher Education Division. He is currently professor in the Humanities/Teacher Education Department at Pepperdine University's Seaver College, Malibu, California. He has written two books, *Creating the Winning Game Plan: The Secondary Teacher's Playbook* (1999) and *Getting Reel: A Social Science Perspective on Film* (2006), as well as numerous articles on teaching, administration, ethics, film, and curriculum change.

Made in the USA
Lexington, KY
10 September 2019